CONTENTS

1. Grimsby to Barton-on-Humber	1-78
2. Barton & Immingham Light Railway	79-81
3. Immingham Dock	82-106
4. Grimsby & Immingham Electric Light Railway	107-120

INDEX

69	Barrow Haven	15	Healing
71	Barton-on-Humber	82	Immingham
79	East Halton Halt	81	Killingholme
12	Great Coates	68	New Holland
38	Goxhill	55	New Holland Pier
107	Grimsby & Immingham Electric Light Railway	48	New Holland Town
		18	Stallingborough
1	Grimsby Town	35	Thornton Abbey
23	Habrough	28	Ulceby

ACKNOWLEDGEMENTS

We are very grateful for the assistance received from many of those mentioned in the credits, also from N.Allsop, A.J.Castledine, G.Croughton, B.S.Doe, G.Gartside, C.M.Howard, S.C.Jenkins, N.Langridge, B.Lewis, Mr D. and Dr S. Salter, T.Walsh and, in particular, our always supportive families.

I. Railway Clearing House route diagram for 1947.

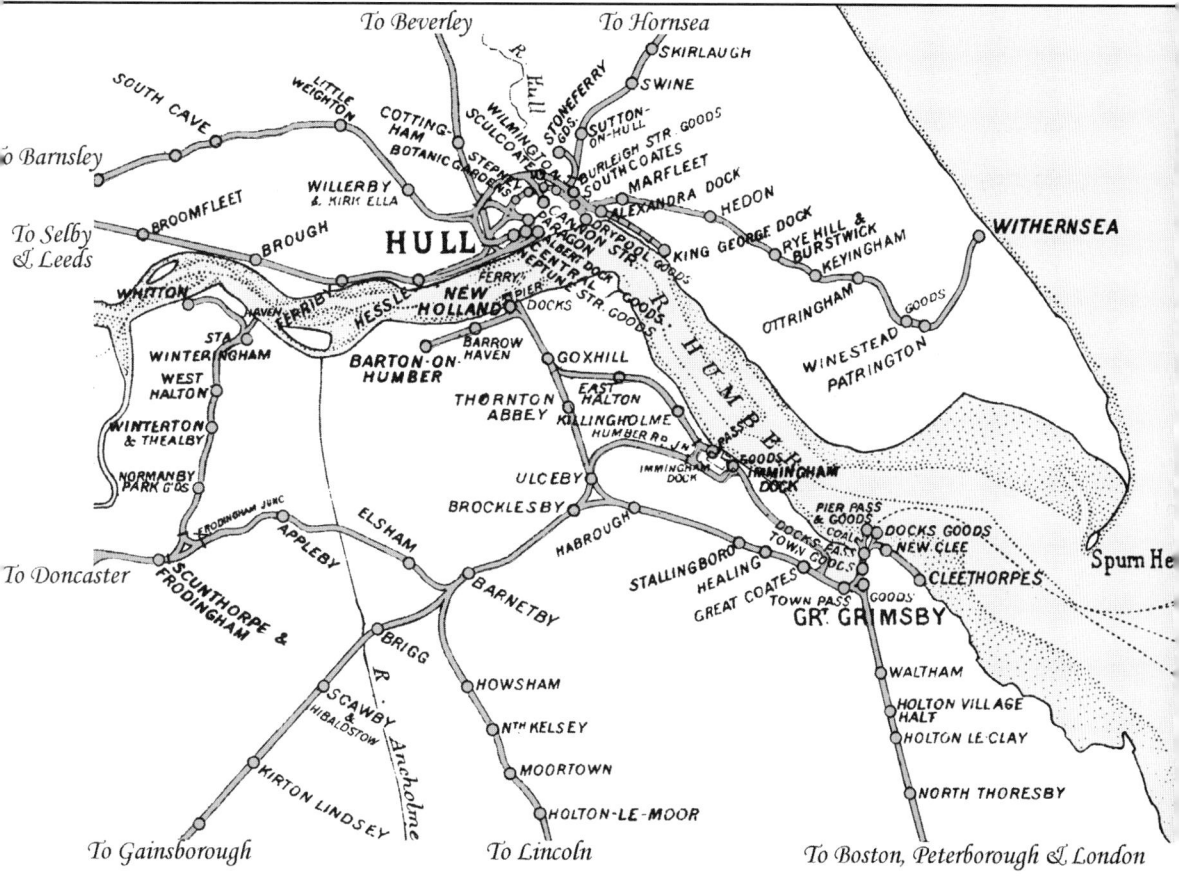

GEOGRAPHICAL SETTING

The entire network herein was constructed on a bed of chalk, through which the Humber Estuary passes. It is west of Barton-on-Humber that a complex group of strata becomes evident.

The district is mostly under 50ft above sea level and the most notable water flow is that of the River Freshney, which reaches the coast at Grimsby Docks. The other important docks are northwest thereof, at Immingham. The routes are entirely within Lincolnshire.

The names of two towns on many early maps are shown as Great Grimsby and Kingston-upon-Hull. The maps are to the scale of 25ins to 1 mile, with north at the top, unless otherwise indicated.

II. The 1946 edition is shown at 4 miles to 1ins. The electric route, between Grimsby and Immingham, has a narrow line with dashes across the fields.

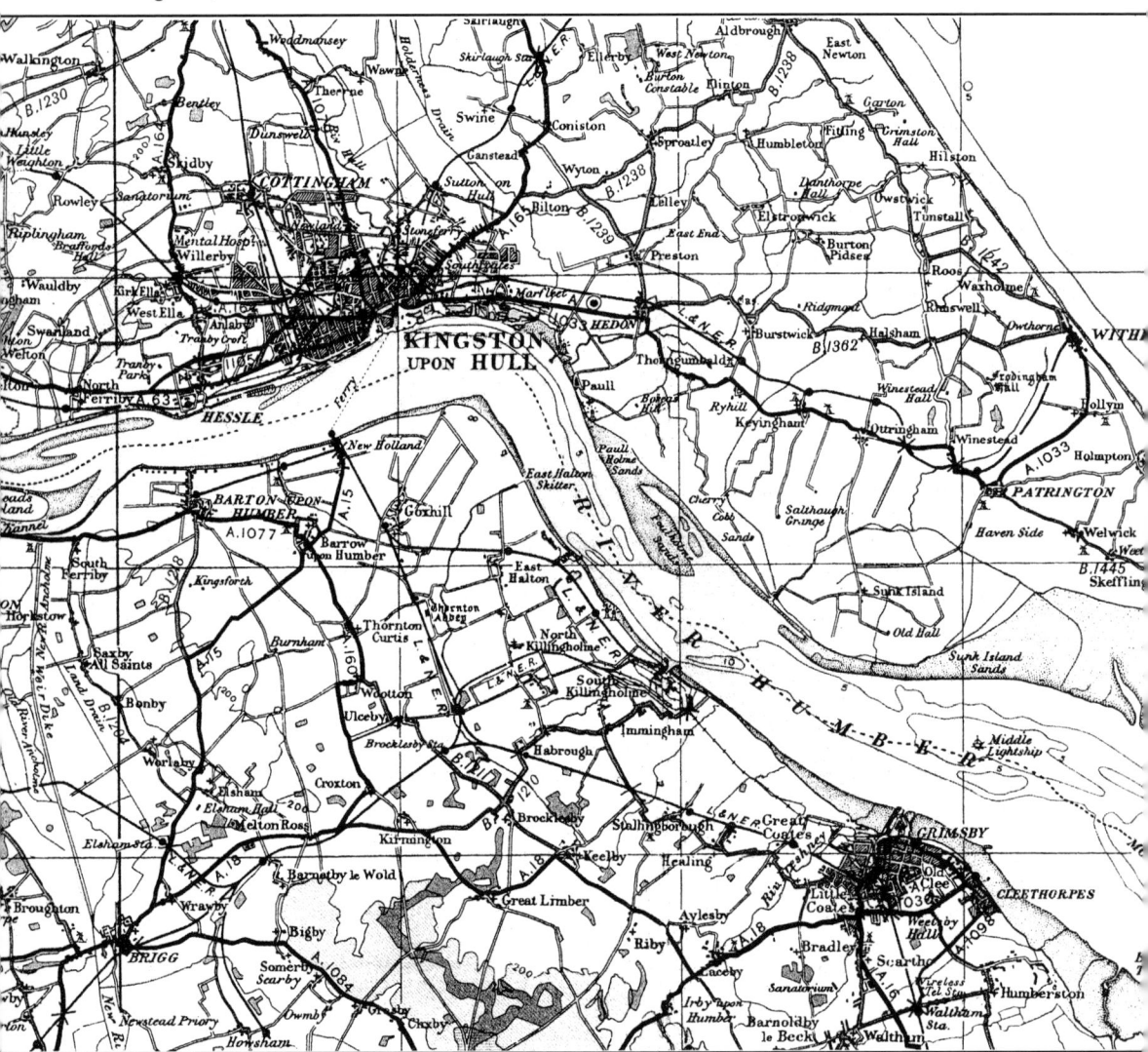

HISTORICAL BACKGROUND

The main line was authorised in 1845 as part of the Great Grimsby & Sheffield Junction Railway, but by the time the line from Grimsby to Lincoln via Market Rasen was opened in 1848, it was part of the Manchester, Sheffield & Lincolnshire (later Great Central) Railway. It opened in three sections: Grimsby to Habrough, Ulceby and New Holland on 1st March, Ulceby and Habrough to Market Rasen (and Brigg) on 1st November and Market Rasen to Lincoln on 18th December. Barton-on-Humber was reached on 1st March 1849. The other company to reach Grimsby was the East Lincolnshire Railway, which ran north from Louth on the same day. The MS&LR extended its network from Grimsby to Cleethorpes on 6th April 1863. The Grimsby to Immingham line was completed in 1906. It was called the Grimsby District Light Railway. Largely parallel to it was the Grimsby & Immingham Electric Railway, which was operated from 15th May 1912 until 1st July 1961, when it closed. However, the 1¼ miles nearest to Grimsby was closed on 30th June 1956.

The railway from Goxhill Junction to Immingham was part of the Barton & Immingham Light Railway, which was acquired by the Humber Commercial Railway & Dock Company and leased to the Great Central Railway, as part of the latter's Immingham Dock project in 1911. It opened from there to Killingholme on 1st December 1910 and on to Goxhill on 1st May 1911. The line west thereof was in the Light Railway Order, but never built. Though the surrounding country was sparsely populated, intermediate stations were provided at East Halton and Killingholme in the hope of further development.

The GCR became part of the London & North Eastern Railway in 1923. This was included in the Eastern Region of British Railways upon nationalisation in 1948. Goods lines are discussed in the captions. New Holland Pier closed on 24th June 1981 to passengers.

Following privatisation, trains to Barton-on-Humber were run by Northern Spirit from 2nd March 1997. It became Arriva Trains Northern on 27th April 2001. A new franchise, called just Northern, commenced on 12th December 2004. Other companies have operated the services inland from Grimsby.

PASSENGER SERVICES

Grimsby to New Holland was the busiest section in the area for many decades. Trains from the south via Louth were supplemented by many from the west of Ulceby. Travellers to Barton had to change at New Holland in the early years. Trains reversed there in later times.

The first two tables offer the complete service northwards in 1850, when combined. The same applies to 1865 and 1906. Bradshaw's staff simplified the presentation later. The timetable extracts continue elsewhere in this album.

Grimsby services in 2017

The station is served on weekdays by TransPennine Express trains between Cleethorpes and Manchester Airport via Sheffield and Manchester Piccadilly (hourly), the Northern-operated Cleethorpes to Barton-on-Humber local stopping service (every two hours) and by East Midlands Trains to Lincoln and Newark (eight trains per day, roughly every two hours). Only the first westbound service each morning and last return pair each evening run to and from Cleethorpes on weekdays - the others all start/terminate here (no through trains to Cleethorpes run on Saturdays). Three Northern trains to and from Sheffield via Retford operate on Saturdays only. Sundays see a two-hourly service to Manchester in the morning, increasing to hourly in the afternoon. A limited service to Barton (four each way) and Lincoln (three each way) operates during the summer months.

LONDON TO HULL, via MIDLAND COUNTIES AND LINCOLN.

Manchester, Sheffield, and Lincolnshire.

Dis. fm. London.	For trains from London and Leicester to Lincoln, page 64; from Birmingham, Derby and Nottingham, to Lincoln, page 61.	Week Days. 1 2 3 clss.	1& 2 clss.	1&2 exp	1 2 3 clss.		Sunday 1 2 3 gov.	1 2 3 gov.	Fares. 1st class.	2nd class.	3rd class.
Mls.		mrn	morn	aft.	aft.		morn	aft.	s. d.	s. d.	s. d.
163½	**Lincoln**........dep.	7 10	9 45	2†30	6 0	..	10 15	5 0	..	..	..
168½	Reepham	7 12	..	..	6 12	..	10 27	5 12	0 10½	0 8	0 5
170	Langworth, for Wragby	7 17	10 0	2 45	6 17	..	10 32	5 17	1 2	0 10½	0 6½
173	Snelland..............	7 25	..	..	6 25	..	10 40	5 25	1 8	1 3½	0 9½
174½	Wickenby............	7 30	10 11	..	6 30	..	10 45	5 30	1 11	1 5½	0 11
178½	**Market Rasen**....	7 41	10 22	3 5	6 41	..	10 56	5 41	2 7½	2 0	1 3
181¼	Usselby	7 49	10 30	..	6 49	..	11 4	5 49	3 0½	2 4	1 5½
184	Holton	7 56	..	..	6 56	..	11 11	5 56	3 7	2 8½	1 8½
185¾	Moortown, for Caistor..	8 1	10 40	3 22	7 1	..	11 16	6 1	3 10	2 10½	1 10
187¼	North Kelsey	8 6	10 45	..	7 6	..	11 21	6 6	4 1	3 1	1 11½
189	Howshsm	8 12	..	..	7 12	..	11 27	6 12	4 5½	3 4½	2 1½
—	**Brigg** ....arr.	8 35	11 12	3 42	7 35	..	11 50	6 35	5 9	4 4	2 9
193	**Barnetby** Junc.dep.	8 23	11 0	3 40	7 23	..	11 38	6 23	..	3 10½	2 5½
197¾	Brocklesby	8 35	11 12	3 52	7 35	..	11 50	6 35	5 11	4 5½	2 10
198¾	**Ulceby** Junc....dep.	8 40	11 17	3 57	7 40	..	11 55	6 40	..	4 7	2 11
201¼	Thornton Abbey	..	..	..	7 45	..	12 0	..	6 6	4 11	3 1½
203	Goxhill	8 51	..	..	7 51	..	12 6	..	6 10½	5 2	3 3½
205¼	**New Holland**... dep.	8 55	11 30	4 10	7 55	..	12 10	6 53	7 2½	5 5½	3 5½
—	**Hull**........... ,,	9 40	12 0	4 40	8 55	..	12 40	7 25	7 8½	5 9½	3 9½

BOSTON to GREAT GRIMSBY, NEW HOLLAND, and HULL.

Dist. frm Boston.	For Stations between Peterbro' and Boston, see below.	Week Days. 1 &2 mail	1 2 3 gov.	1 2 3 gov.	1 & 2 class.	1 &2 clss.	1 &2 exp.	1 &2 clss.	Sundays. 1 &2 mail	1 2 3 gov.	1 2 3 gov.	1 2 3 gov.	Fares. From Grimsby. 1st clss.	2nd class.	3rd class.
Mls.		mrn	mrn	mrn	morn	aft.	aft.	aft.	mrn	mrn	aft.	aft.	s. d.	s. d.	s. d.
—	**Boston** ......dep.	2 44	..	6 50	9‡20	1 45	4 6	5 39	2 44	..	2 4	..			
—	Sibsey............	..	..	7 3	9 33	1 58	..	5 52	..	..	2 17	..	..	..	..
—	Old Leake & Wrangle	..	..	7 9	9 39	2 4	..	5 58	..	..	2 23	..	..	..	..
—	East Ville & New Leak	..	..	7 17	9 47	2 12	..	6 6	..	..	2 31	..	..	..	..
—	Little Steeping......	..	..	7 25	9 55	2 20	..	6 14	..	..	2 49	..	..	..	..
—	**Firsby**, Spilsby, &c.	3 16	..	7 36	10 6	2 31	4 37	6 25	3 16	..	2 51	..	..	..	..
—	**Burgh**............	..	..	7 42	10 12	2 37	4 43	6 31	..	..	2 57	..	..	..	..
—	Willoughby	..	..	7 52	10 22	2 47	..	6 41	..	..	3 7	..	..	..	..
—	**Alford**	3 32	..	8 3	10 33	2 58	4 58	6 52	3 32	..	3 18	..	..	..	..
—	Claythorpe..........	..	..	8 11	10 41	3 6	..	7 0	..	..	3 26	..	..	..	..
—	Authorpe	..	..	8 15	10 45	3 10	..	7 4	..	..	3 30	..	..	..	..
—	Legbourne..........	..	..	8 25	10 55	3 20	..	7 14	..	..	3 40	..	..	..	..
—	**Louth**............	3 52	..	8 36	11 6	3 31	5 20	7 25	3 52	..	3 51	..	..	..	..
—	Ludborough	..	..	8 48	11 18	3 43	..	7 37	..	..	4 3	..	..	..	..
—	**North Thoresby**	..	..	8 54	11 22	3 49	..	7 43	..	..	4 9	..	..	..	..
—	Holton-le-Clay & Tet.	..	..	9 0	11 30	3 55	..	7 49	..	..	4 15	..	..	..	..
—	Waltham & Humbrstn	..	..	9 6	11 36	4 1	..	7 55	..	..	4 21	..	..	..	..
—	**Gt. Grimsby** dep	4 23	6 45	9†18	11*49	4*13	5 50	8 11	4 23	6 45	4 38	6 5	..	..	..
—	Great Coates........	..	6 51	9 24	11 55	4 19	..	8 17	..	6 51	4 44	6 11	0 6	0 4	0 2
—	Stallingborough	..	6 57	9 30	12 1	4 25	..	8 23	..	6 57	4 50	6 17	0 9	0 6½	0 4
—	Habrough	..	7 6	9 39	12 10	4 34	..	8 32	..	7 6	4 59	6 26	1 5	1 1	0 8
—	**Ulceby Junc.** dep	4 43	7 11	9 47	12 15	4 42	6 10	8 40	4 43	7 16	5 7	6 37	1 8	1 3½	0 9½
—	Thornton Abbey	..		..	..	..	..	..	..	..	..	..	2 1½	1 7	1 0
—	Goxhill	..	..	9 56	12 27	4 51	..	8 49	..	7 26	5 16	6 46	2 5½	1 10	1 2
—	**New Holland** arr	4 55	..	10 0	12 31	4 55	6 25	8 53	4 55	7 30	5 20	6 50	2 9½	2 1½	1 4
—	**Hull** .... ,,	5 25	..	1030	1 10	5 25	6 55	9 20	5 25	8 0	5 50	7 25	3 3½	2 5½	1 8

*1 2 3 gov. from Gt. Grimsby. †1 & 2 class from Gt. Grimsby. ‡ Gov. train for passengers from Great Northern Railway.

March 1850

November 1865

CLEETHORPES, GREAT GRIMSBY, NEW HOLLAND, and HULL.—Manchester, Sheffield, and Lincolnshire.

Miles.	From Peterbro', Boston, &c., see page 87.	Week Days. 1,2,3 gov	1,2,3 gov	1&2 b	1&2 d	1,2,3 aft	1,2,3 gov	1&2 e	1,2,3 ad	1,2,3 aft	Sundays. 1,2,3 gov	1,2,3 gov	1,2,3 gov	1,2,3 gvd	
—	**Cleethorps** d	f	a	9 15	1230	2 0	Mon. Fri.	4 30	7 35	9 40	a	10 0	4 0	..	..
2½	Grimsby Docks.	6 0	6 35	9 22	1237	2 8		4 41	7 43	9 50	7 35	10 8	4 10	7 35	..
3¾	**Grimsby** ar	6 5	6 40	9 26	1242	2 12		4 49	7 47	..	7 40	1012	4 14	7 40	..
	87 dp	6 15	6 45	9 40	1250	2 25	3 30	5 5	8 5	..	7 45	1040	4 25	7 55	..
5¼	Great Coates....	6 20	6 51	9 46	..	c	3 36	5 11	8 10	..	7 51	1046	..	8 1	..
7½	Stallingbro'	6 25	6 57	9 52	1 0	2 35	3 48	5 17	8 16	..	7 57	1052	4 34	8 7	..
11½	Habrough	6 35	7 7	10 0	..	2 43	4 4	5 26	8 26	..	8 7	11 2	4 43	8 16	..
13	**Ulceby**.. arr	6 40	7 11	10 4	1 14	2 47	4 12	5 30	8 30	..	8 11	11 7	4 47	8 20	..
	174 dep	..	7 14	1010	1 25	2 48	4 16	5 33	8 45	..	8 13	1110	4 49	8 28	..
5½	Thornton Abbey.	..	7 20	..	..	..	4 21	5 39	..	..	8 20	1116	..	8 34	..
17½	Goxhill	..	7 24	1020	..	..	4 24	5 44	..	..	8 25	1120	..	8 40	..
19½	**N. Holland** 170		7 30	1025	1 35	3 0	4 31	5 50	9 0	..	8 30	1125	5 0	8 45	..
—	**Hull** 164,165,166a		8 0	1055	2 0	3 30	..	6 20	9 30	..	9 0	1245	5 30	9 15	..

For Nrth Eastern arrivals, 164 & 165	Week Days. 1,2,3 gvd	1,2,3 a	1&2 mrn	1,2,3 gva	1,2,3 d	1&2 aft	1&2 aft	1,2,3 gov	1,2,3 aft	Sundays. 1,2,3 gva	1,2,3 gov	1 2 g aft	1,2,3 gov	1,2,3 gov
Corporation Pier, **Hull** ......dep	6 0	8 15	9 30	1110	1240	3 45	Saturdays only	6 40	..	8 15	1110	4 25	6 40	..
N. Holland..	6 30	8 45	9 58	1140	1 10	4 15		7 10	..	8 45	1140	4 55	7 10	..
Goxhill	6 36	..	..	1145	1 16	..		7 15	..	8 51	1146	5 1	7 16	..
Thornton Abbey.	6 41	..	..	1149	1 21	..		c	..	8 55	1151	..	7 21	..
Ulceby Junc..... arr	6 46	8 55	1010	1155	1 26	4 25		7 23	..	9 2	1155	5 9	7 25	..
dep	7 12	8 56	..	1158	1 40	4 26	5 15	7 27	8 52	9 4	1158	Stop	7 29	8 40
Habrough	7 17	9 0	..	12 3	1 45	4 31		7 32	8 57	9 8	12 4		7 34	8 46
Stallingbro'	7 27	9 10	..	1213	1 55	4 40		7 41	9 7	9 17	1214		7 44	8 56
Great Coates	7 32	9 15	..	1220	c	c		c	c	9 23	1220	1,2,3	7 50	c
Grimsby ar	7 36	9 20	..	1225	2 7	4 50	5 55	7 52	9 15	9 28	1225	gov	7 55	9 5
87 dp	7 40	9 30	..	1235	2 25	5 10	..	8 5	9 17	9 35	1230	2 0	8 0	9 7
Grimsby Docks..	7 45	9 35	..	1240	2 30	5 15	..	8 10	9 21	9 39	1235	2 5	8 5	9 12
Cleethorpes	7 52	9 42	..	1248	2 38	5 22	..	..	..	9 46	1242	2 12	..	..

a 3rd class between Hull and Grimsby, Fare, 1s. **b** 3rd class from Cleethorpes to Grimsby Docks, Grimsby, and Hull. **c** Stop when required. **d** Change carriages at Ulceby. **e** 3rd class from Cleethorpes, Grimsby Docks, and Grimsby to Hull only. **f** Starts from Cleethorpes on Mondays at 6 mrn.

LINCOLN, MARKET RASEN, and HULL.—Manchester, Sheffield, and Lincolnshire.

Fares. 1 cl.	2 cl.	3 cl.	From Scarbro' & Bridlington, 165	Week Days. 1,2,3 gov	1&2 exp	1,2,3 f	1&2 b	1,2,3 aft	Sndys 123g a	1,2,3 gov
s. d.	s. d.	s. d.	Corporation Pier, **Hull** ......dep	7 0	9 30	9 30	1240	5 0	8 15	4 25
..	..	..								
0 6	0 4	0 4	**Nw Holland**	7 30	9 58	1010	1 10	5 45	8 50	5 15
1 0	0 8	0 7	Goxhill	7 36	..	1016	1 16	5 52	8 56	5 22
1 5	0 11	0 9	Thornton Abbey.	7 41	..	..	1 21	5 57	9 2	5 27
1 11	1 4	1 0	Ulceby .... arr	7 46	1010	1023	1 26	6 5	9 7	5 32
			dep	7 49	1012	1025	1 27	6 8	9 10	5 36
2 2	1 6	1 2	Brocklesby	7 53	1016	1029	1 30	6 12	9 14	5 41
3 2	2 2	1 8	Barnetby .. arr	8 4	1025	1039	1 40	6 22	9 24	5 51
			dep	8 6	1027	1041	1 42	6 25	9 31	5 54
4 0	2 10	2 0	Howsham	8 15	Via Retford.	1050	1 51	d	9 41	6 4
4 5	3 0	2 4	North Kelsey....	8 20		1057	1 57	6 39	9 47	6 10
4 9	3 4	2 6	Moortown, frCais-	8 25		11 3	2 3	6 44	9 52	6 15
5 1	3 6	2 8	Holton ......[tor	8 30		11 8	2 8	6 50	9 57	6 20
5 9	4 0	3 0	Usselby	8 37		1115	2 15	d	10 4	6 27
6 5	4 6	3 4	**Mrkt Rasen**	8 45		1123	2 23	7 6	1010	6 33
7 4	5 0	3 10	Wickenby	8 54		1133	2 32	7 16	1021	6 45
7 6	5 4	3 10	Snelland	8 59		..	2 38	7 21	1027	6 50
8 2	5 8	4 2	Lngwrth, Wragby	9 7		1145	2 46	7 29	1035	6 58
8 7	6 0	4 4	Reepham [174.87	9 12		..	2 50	Tu.	1040	7 3
9 8	6 10	4 10	**Lincoln 156**, a	9 22	1 0	12 0	3 0	7 45	1050	7 15
15 11	11 6	6 6½	156 Nottinghm ar	1145	2 20	..	5 50	9 10	..	9 10
17 11	13 0	7 8½	Derby 156 ,,	1240	3 5	..	6 55	9 55	..	9 55

	Week Days. mrn	mrn	aft	aft	Sndys mrn	mrn
156 Derby ..dep	3 5	6 50	1 5	2 45	3 5	7 45
156 Nottinghm ,,	3 49	7 55	1 55	3 40	3 49	8 35
From Boston, 87; from Derby, 156.	1,2,3 c	1&2 b	1&2 aft	1,2,3 gov	123g c	1,2,3 gov
Lincoln ..dep	5 45	10 5	3 30	6 45	6 30	3 0
Reepham........	5 55	Tu.	3 40	6 57	6 42	3 12
Lngwrth, Wragby	6 0	1019	3 45	7 2	6 47	3 17
Snelland	6 7	1026	3 52	7 10	6 55	3 25
Wickenby	..	1030	3 56	7 15	7 0	3 30
Mrkt Rasen	6 19	1040	4 6	7 26	7 11	3 41
Usselby	6 26	Tu.	4 13	7 34	7 19	3 49
Holton ......[tor	6 33	1052	4 20	7 41	7 26	3 56
Moortown, frCais-	6 38	1057	4 25	7 46	7 31	4 1
North Kelsey....	g	11 1	4 29	7 51	7 36	4 6
Howsham	6 45	11 6	4 35	7 57	7 42	4 12
Barnetby .. arr	6 52	1115	4 43	8 5	7 50	4 20
174 dep	6 53	1118	4 45	8 7	7 52	4 22
Brocklesby	7 3	1126	4 56	8 18	8 3	4 33
Ulceby **175**......	7 6	1130	5 1	8 22	8 7	4 37
Thornton Abbey..	..	1136	5 8	8 29	8 20	4 44
Goxhill.... [170	..	..	5 14	8 35	8 25	4 50
N. Holland ar	7 20	1145	5 20	8 40	8 30	4 55
Hull 164,165,,	8 0	1215	6 20	9 20	9 10	5 30

a Change at Barnetby. **b** Stop at Bigby Road Bridge, on Thursdays, when required. **c** Change at Ulceby. **d** Stops when required. **f** Fridays only, calling at Bigby Road Bridge. **g** Stops on Tuesdays and Fridays, when required.

HULL, NEW HOLLAND, BROCKLESBY, GRIMSBY, and CLEETHORPES.—Great Central.

July 1906

Timetable showing Up and Down weekday and Sunday services between Hull (Corporation Pier), New Holland, Goxhill, Thornton Abbey, Ulceby, Brocklesby, Habrough, Stallingboro', Healing, Great Coates, Grimsby Town (355), Grimsby Docks, New Clee, and Cleethorpes.

Notes:
- **a** Stops to take up for Barnetby or beyond on notice being given at the Station.
- **b** Passengers for Grimsby change at Brocklesby.
- **c** Stops to set down 1st class Passengers on informing the Guard at New Holland.
- **d** Passengers for Hull change at Brocklesby.
- **f** Stop to take up for Barnetby or beyond on notice being given at the Station.
- **g** Stop to take up on notice being given at the Station.

Sundays
- **a** Stop when required to take up on notice being given at the Station.
- **b** Passengers for Grimsby change at Brocklesby.
- **g** Runs via Barton.

CLEETHORPES, GRIMSBY, HULL, MARKET RASEN, and LINCOLN.—Great Central.

Timetable showing Down and Up weekday and Sunday services between Cleethorpes, New Clee, Grimsby Docks, Grimsby Town, Great Coates, Healing, Stallingboro', Habrough, 694 Hull (Cor. Pr.), 694 New Holland, Brocklesby, Barnetby, Howsham, North Kelsey, Moortown for Caistor, Holton, Claxby and Usselby, Market Rasen, Wickenby, Snelland, Langworth for Wragby, Reepham, and Lincoln* 319, 364.

Notes:
- **a** Stops when required to take up 1st class Passengers for beyond Barnetby.
- **c** Stop to take up on notice being given at the Station.
- **d** Passengers to and from Grimsby change at Barnetby.
- **f** Stops to set down from Lincoln on informing the Guard at Lincoln.
- **g** Stops to set down from Barnetby or beyond on notice being given to the Guard at Barnetby.
- ***** Great Northern Station.

1. Grimsby to Barton-on-Humber

GRIMSBY TOWN

III. The Royal Dock opened in 1852 and it was connected to Old Dock, which was south of Lock Hill, in 1873. Thus, Union Dock came into being and Alexandra Dock was developed. The connection southwards to the main line at Great Coates followed in 1879. This became one of the busiest fishing ports in the world and refrigeration facilities eventually followed. Further important progress came in 2013 when a jetty for roll on/roll off ships opened. The Emigrants Home is marked on this 1950 map at 6ins to 1 mile. It has Docks Station and Goods Shed marked on the right of the left page. Town Station was just beyond its lower border and is in detail overleaf, on map IV. New Clee station is on the right page, together with the line to Cleethorpes and the extra fish docks from the 1930s. Inset top right is a 1908 extract at 5ins to 1 mile, with Town Station lower centre. Victoria Street makes the connection between it and the left page of the main map. Trains to Peterborough used the line at the lower end of the triangle.

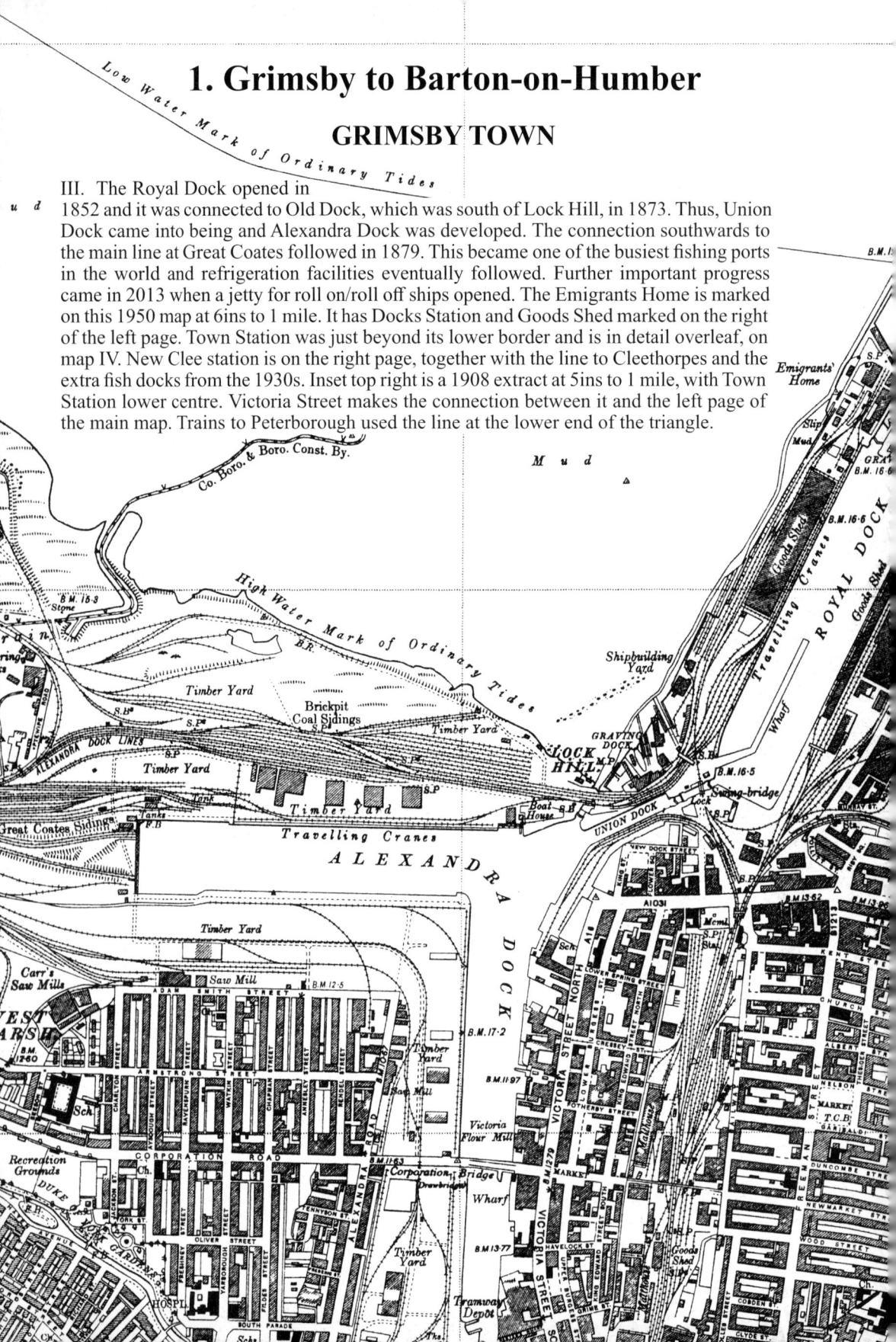

1. The first station was the terminus of a branch from the main line from Gainsborough to New Holland at Ulceby. It helped the town grow enormously. The docks also grew rapidly, handling mainly coal outwards and fish inwards. The tonnage of fish landed here grew from 71,000 tons in 1891 to almost 180,000 by 1910. Most of it left by rail. This station was near the Old Market Place and was demolished at an unknown date. Its successor had three tracks under a wider roof. (R.Humm coll.)

2. In the early years, many of the passengers were migrants going from mainland Europe to America, taking single tickets from here to Liverpool after arriving. In railway parlance, these passengers were known as transmigrants. Through trains were run after 1888, when the direct connection to Brocklesby came into use. On the right of this 1960 view of Town station is one of Sugg's Rochester style shadow-free gas lamps. (R.Humm coll.)

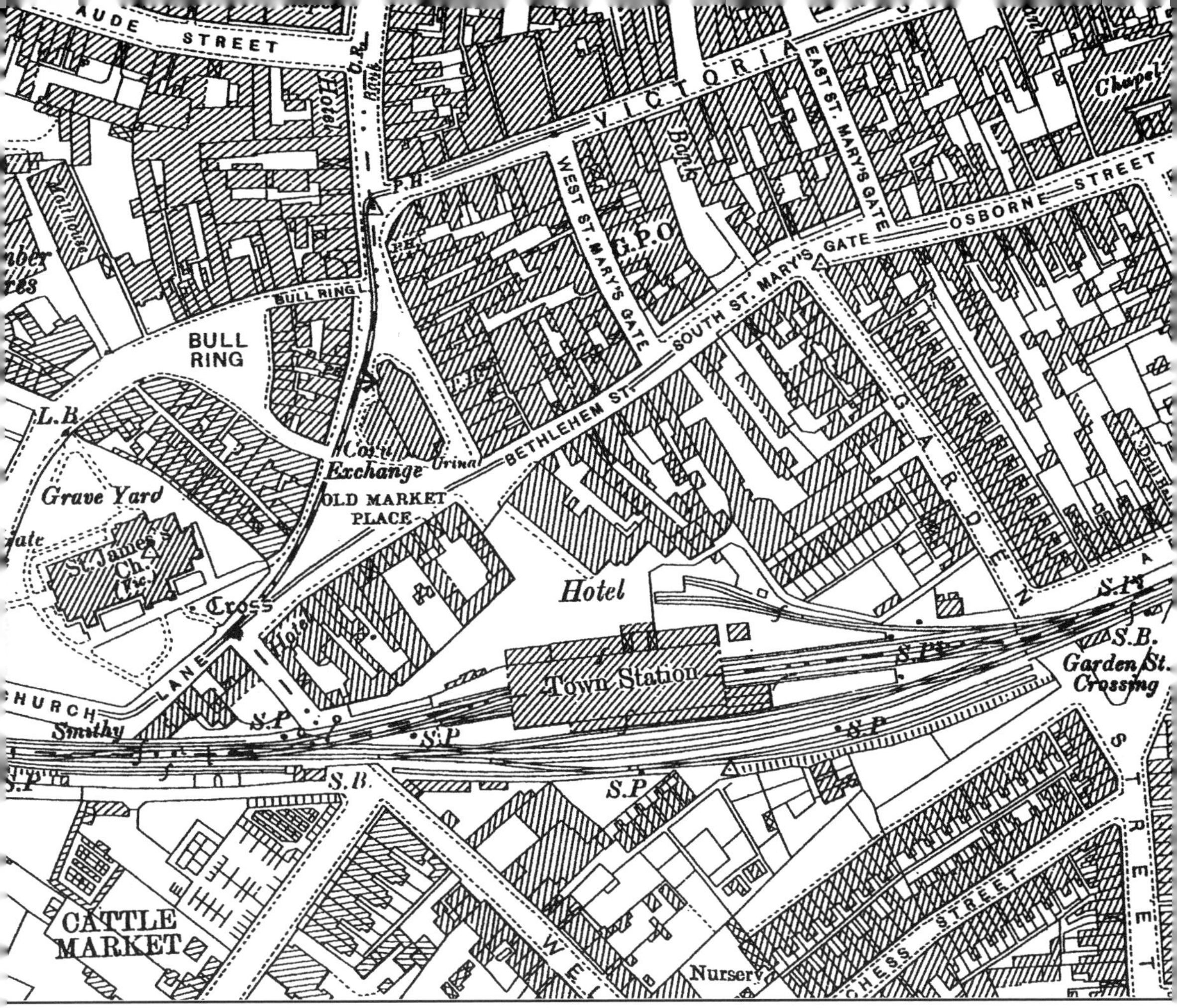

IV. The 1906 edition includes the Grimsby Corporation Tramways, which started in 1881 with horses and was electrified in 1901. It was extended to Cleethorpes, but closed entirely in 1937.

3. Both trains carry rear lamps, because the right track had bi-directional working. A serious railway student has found a firm observation position; his back is to a new Jaguar. This view is also from 1960, the year in which the station became electrically lit. (R.Humm coll.)

4. Hotel windows overlook the west end and most movements could be observed from them, except down trains terminating at platform 3. A DMU stands at it; Lincoln and Doncaster services used it regularly. (J.Alsop coll.)

5. The suffix TOWN was added in 1900. This fine westward panorama is from about 1970 and it includes Wellowgate level crossing, plus its signal box. Beyond it was the triangular junction for trains running south to Peterborough or north to Grimsby Docks station and Cleethorpes. (LOSA)

6. Two wide angle views from 17th March 1981 record the location well. This was taken from close to Wellowgate level crossing. Its barriers were controlled under CCTV from Pasture Street Box from 29th September 1993. (D.A.Thompson)

> **Other views of this area can be seen in our** *Lincoln to Cleethorpes* **album and the** *Spalding to Grimsby* **volume.** *Grimsby & Cleethorpes Trolleybuses* **also contains much of local interest.**

7. This is the north elevation and beyond the wall on the left had been two short sidings, with docks, which are shown on the last map. Public goods traffic here ceased on 2nd August 1965. Nearer to the Docks station was Pasture Street Depot, which was in use until 2nd October 1972. (D.A.Thompson)

8. It is 30th November 2006 and no. 185134 has arrived at platform 2 with the 13.28 Cleethorpes-Manchester Airport. Note the interior footbridge under the new roof, which was fitted with a shelter over the centre part of the bridge. The old walls had been retained. All three platforms could take seven cars. Annual passenger figures exceeded 0.420m in 2011-16. (A.C.Hartless)

9. The class 20s were on a rail head treatment train, which jets a high-power water spray along the rail to wash off the leaf contamination in the autumn. This was the 08.52 Wakefield Wrenthorpe to Grimsby. It normally ran three times a week from early October to the first week of December, depending on leaf fall. The locos are in 'top and tail' formation; no. 20309 is on the front and no. 20302 at the rear. They were operated by Direct Rail Services and based in York for the leaf fall season. The service then ran to Malton. The three tank wagons contain water for the high-speed jetting and had to be replenished at the end of the circuit. (R.Geach)

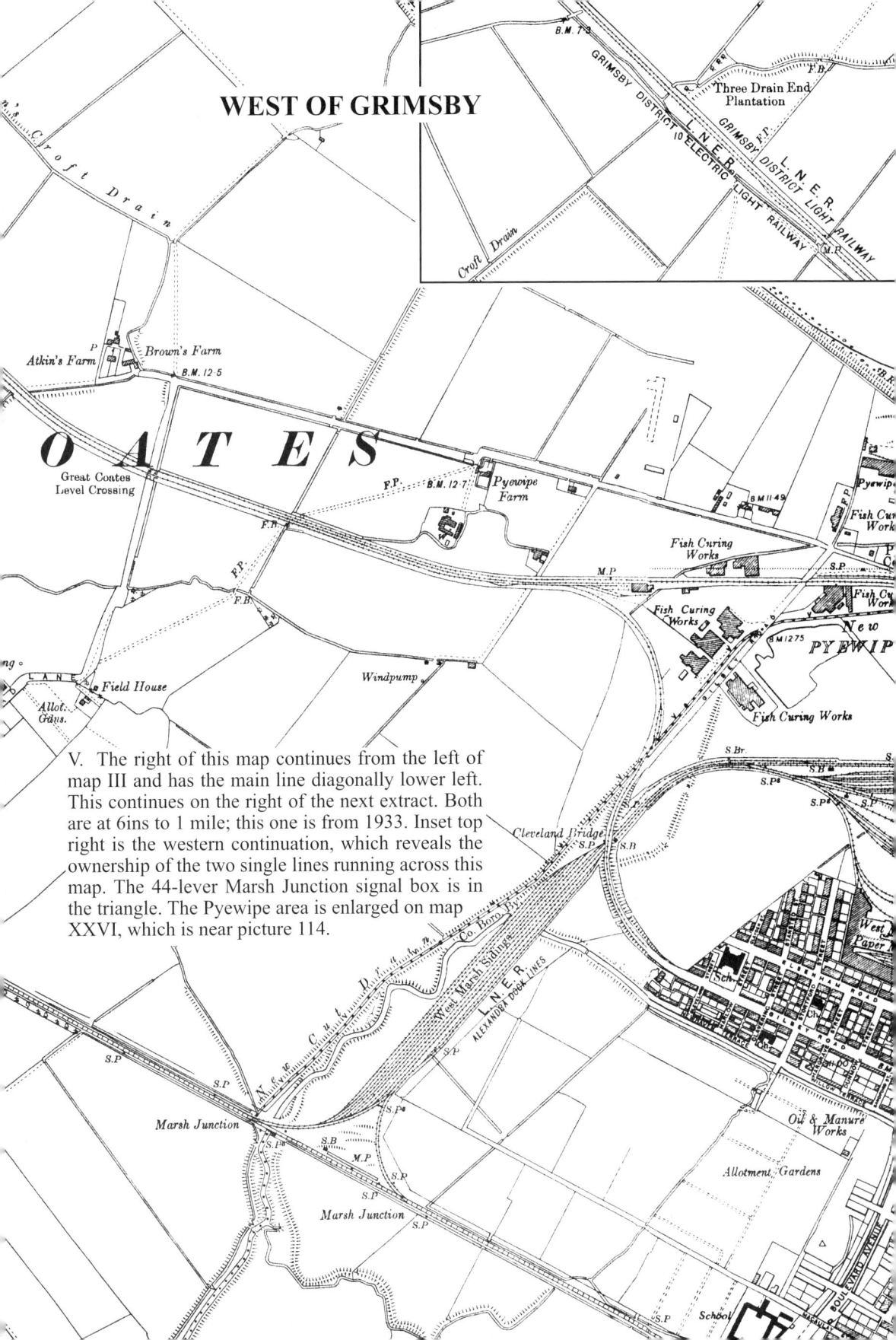

WEST OF GRIMSBY

V. The right of this map continues from the left of map III and has the main line diagonally lower left. This continues on the right of the next extract. Both are at 6ins to 1 mile; this one is from 1933. Inset top right is the western continuation, which reveals the ownership of the two single lines running across this map. The 44-lever Marsh Junction signal box is in the triangle. The Pyewipe area is enlarged on map XXVI, which is near picture 114.

10. Grimsby West Marsh sidings had once been busy with freight to and from Grimsby Docks, but little traffic remained by the 1980s. A visit on 12th April 1983 finds no. 31195 with a solitary brake van on local trip duties and resident shunter no. 08743. A few tank wagons and steel flats loaded with coil wait on the far side. Marsh Junction signal box is visible in the triangle of lines giving access from the main line to West Marsh sidings. The box was closed under the Grimsby area resignalling scheme of 2015-16. The line through West Marsh sidings was then technically still open, but rarely used. (P.D.Shannon)

11. No. 4771 *Green Arrow* has passed West Marsh sidings and has just run under Cleveland Bridge on 3rd March 2007, while hauling the Railway Touring Company's 'The Great Central'. The train ran from and back to Kings Cross via Peterborough. The class V2 2-6-2 had for long been BR no. 60800. The box is Great Coates No. 1. The bridge is shown right of centre on the last map seen. (J.Whitehouse)

GREAT COATES

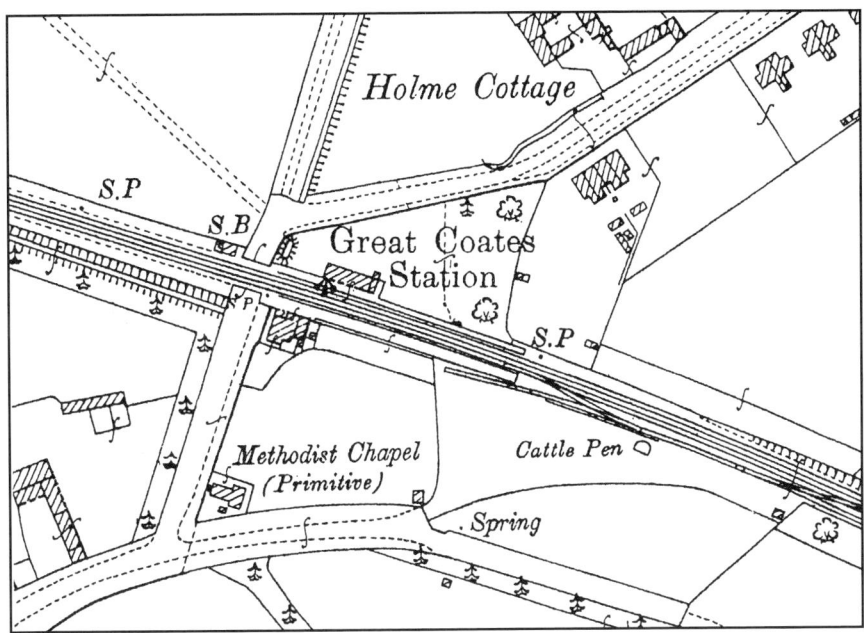

VI. The 1906 edition shows the goods loop and the unusual shape of the goods yard. Its gate is near the Spring and its traffic ceased on 25th May 1964. The population was only 294 in 1901.

For other pictures, see nos 74-77 in *Lincoln to Cleethorpes.*

12. The 1884 signal box had a 39-lever frame. It was in service until 18th October 1987, by when automatic half barriers were in use on the level crossing. Staffing ceased on 29th June 1969. (J.Alsop coll.)

13. A view from the 1950s includes the extensive accommodation for the station master and his family. As was common for generations, the facilities for gentlemen were devoid of a roof. (D.K.Jones coll.)

14. Northern Rail's no. 153316 arrives with the 11.58 Barton-on-Humber to Cleethorpes on 30th November 2006. The right platform took four cars and the other, three. There are identical shelters on both platforms. Annually, passengers numbered 9000 to 11,500 from 2013 to 2016. (A.C.Hartless)

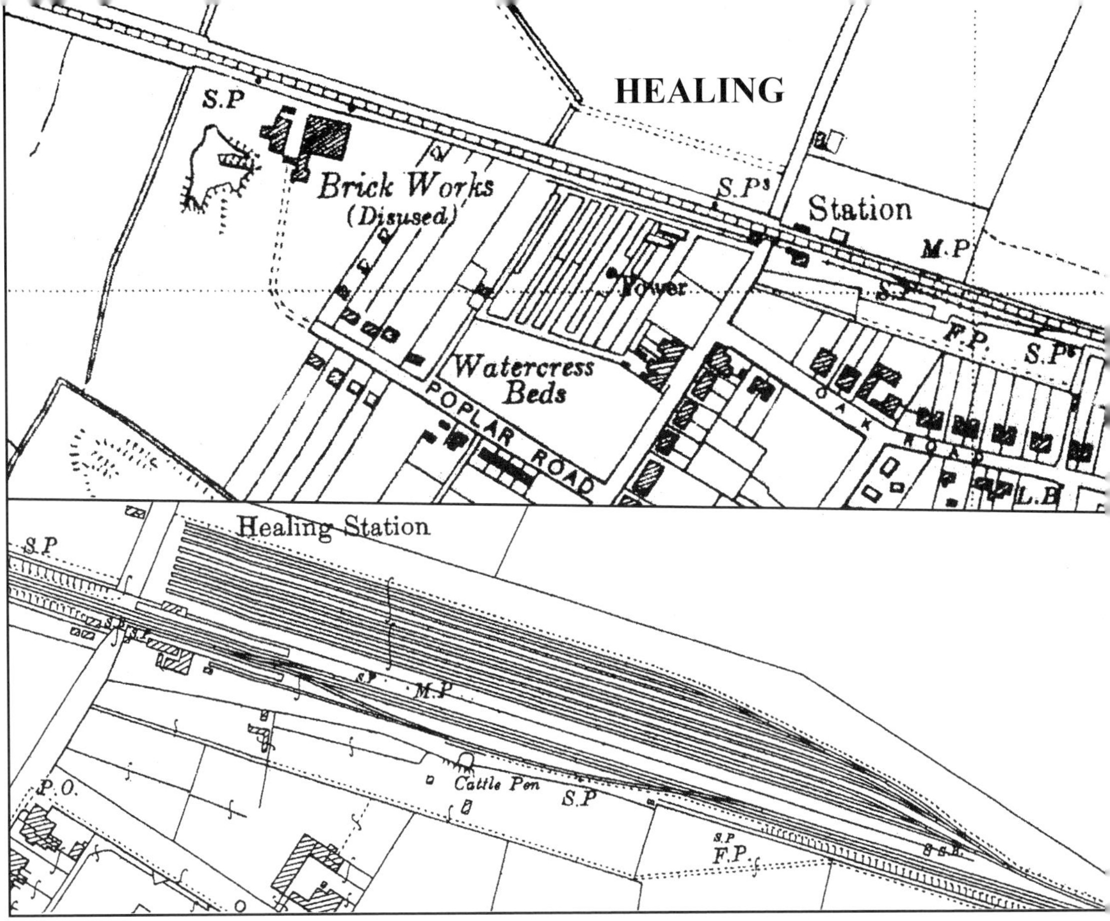

VII. The upper map is from 1946 and is at 6ins to 1 mile. It includes one of many watercress beds in the district. Below it is a 1906 extract at 20ins to 1 mile, which features nine sidings for holding coal wagons awaiting transfer to the docks. Lower down is the goods yard, which closed on 27th April 1964.

15. This station opened later than most on the route, on 1st April 1881. It is seen in the Victorian era, when heads and ankles should not be uncovered. The train is running in from the west, with some of the coal wagons standing on the right. (P.Laming coll.)

16. The station ceased to be staffed on 29th June 1969 and is seen shortly before that. Gas lamps had to be lit and extinguished by station staff. There seems to have been a case of neglect of duty. (LOSA)

> **For other pictures of Healing, see nos 72 and 73 in *Lincoln to Cleethorpes*.**

17. It is 17th July 2014 and the 13.26 Cleethorpes-Manchester Airport service, formed of two-car units nos 170309 and 170303, runs through. The up side building has been retiled and refenestrated, but was no longer in railway use. The dustbin liner outside the shelter indicates the draught from the speeding train. Passengers numbered 12,260 in 2013-14. (A.C.Hartless)

STALLINGBOROUGH

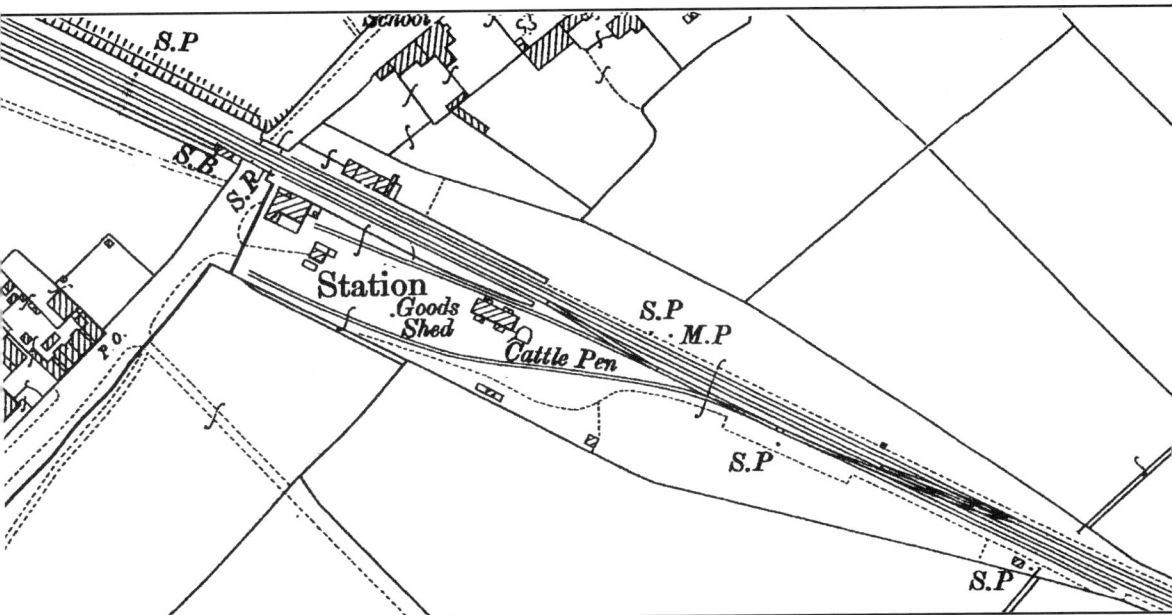

VIII. The 1906 edition reveals the extent of the goods yard, which was in use until 25th May 1964. North of the station was the school, the Manor House and a two-mile walk to the coast.

18. We look west in this undated view, which may be from the 1970s. Staffing ceased in 1969 and there are now no helpful signs to be seen. Residents totalled 420 in 1901. (J.Alsop coll.)

19. The 1884 20-lever box was photographed on 18th August 1974, when it still controlled wooden gates using a rare cast iron wheel. The box was replaced by a new one in 2007, following serious ground settlement. (R.Humm coll.)

> **For other pictures of this station, see nos 70 and 71 in** *Lincoln to Cleethorpes*.

20. The new box was recorded on 6th May 2010, when both platforms could take four coaches. The building was completed in 2007 and a panel controlled new colour light signals and barriers. (R.Humm)

WEST OF STALLINGBOROUGH

21. This is the scene one mile from the station on 3rd June 1962, when one of the first UK lifting barriers came into use. They were on the B1210 road to Little London and were half barriers. (R.Humm coll.)

22. A further mile west was the 1883 Roxton Sidings Box, which was pictured on 26th July 1988. Earlier maps had termed the location 'Immingham Sidings'. The box is on the north side of the route and was still in use in 2016. It once had a quarry nearby and was fitted with an 18-lever frame, plus a small gate wheel. (R.Humm)

HABROUGH

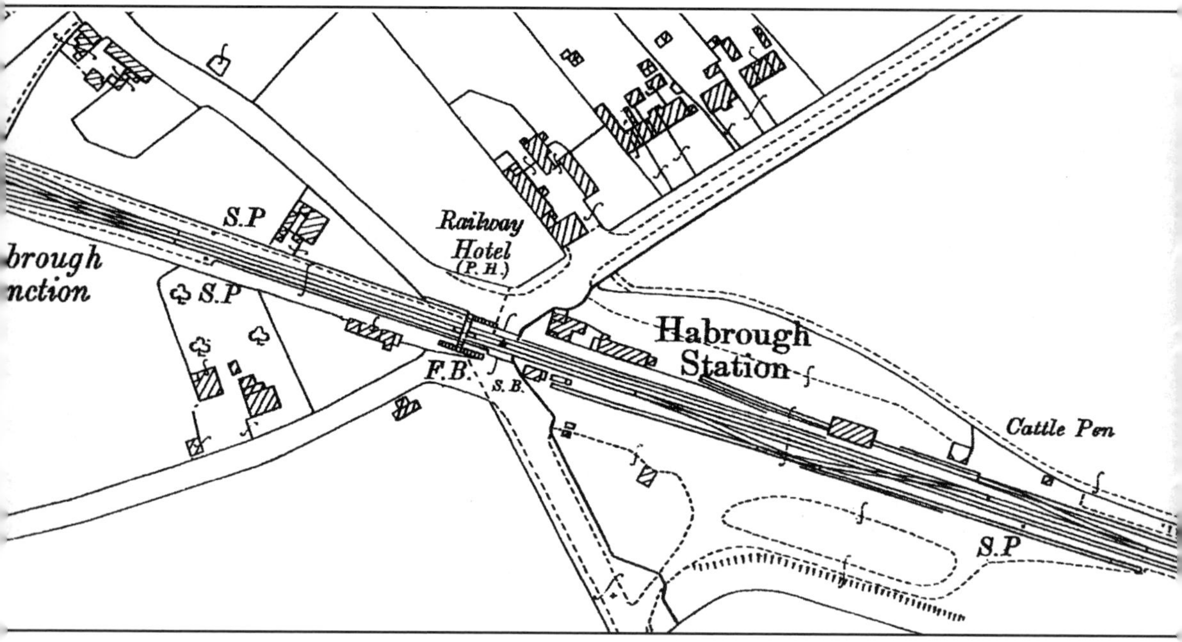

IX. This 1906 extract features goods facilities both sides of the running lines and cross roads at the level crossing. Both yards have curvaceous boundaries. The census in 1901 showed 344 living here.

23. This westward panorama clearly shows that the platforms are staggered and separated by the level crossing and footbridge. Seldom are all the goods shed doors over its siding seen open in a photograph. (P.Laming coll.)

24. LNER class D9 4-4-0 no. 6024 is passing the goods dock on 4th August 1934, with a New Holland to Cleethorpes train. This class was built in 1901-04. (R.Humm coll.)

25. A DMU from Cleethorpes is slowing down as it enters the down platform on 27th July 1979. The gates were worked by a large wheel in the box and complex mechanisms, some of which can be seen in the foreground. The box had 28 levers and was in use from 1883 to 18th September 1988. (T.Heavyside)

26. Calling on 5th June 1980 are class 114 cars E56003, E50009, E50032 and E56007 with a train bound for Doncaster. Although track layout seems to give equal importance to the Doncaster and New Holland lines, the positioning of the semaphore arms shows that the Doncaster line is the major route. (P.D.Shannon)

27. It is 30th November 2006 and no. 185139 approaches with the 11.52 Manchester Airport-Cleethorpes. The platforms are still staggered either side of the level crossing of the B1210. The once substantial down side building has been replaced by a small shelter. Passengers numbered just 30,000 annually in 2011-16. (A.C.Hartless)

For other pictures, see nos 64-69 in *Lincoln to Cleethorpes*.

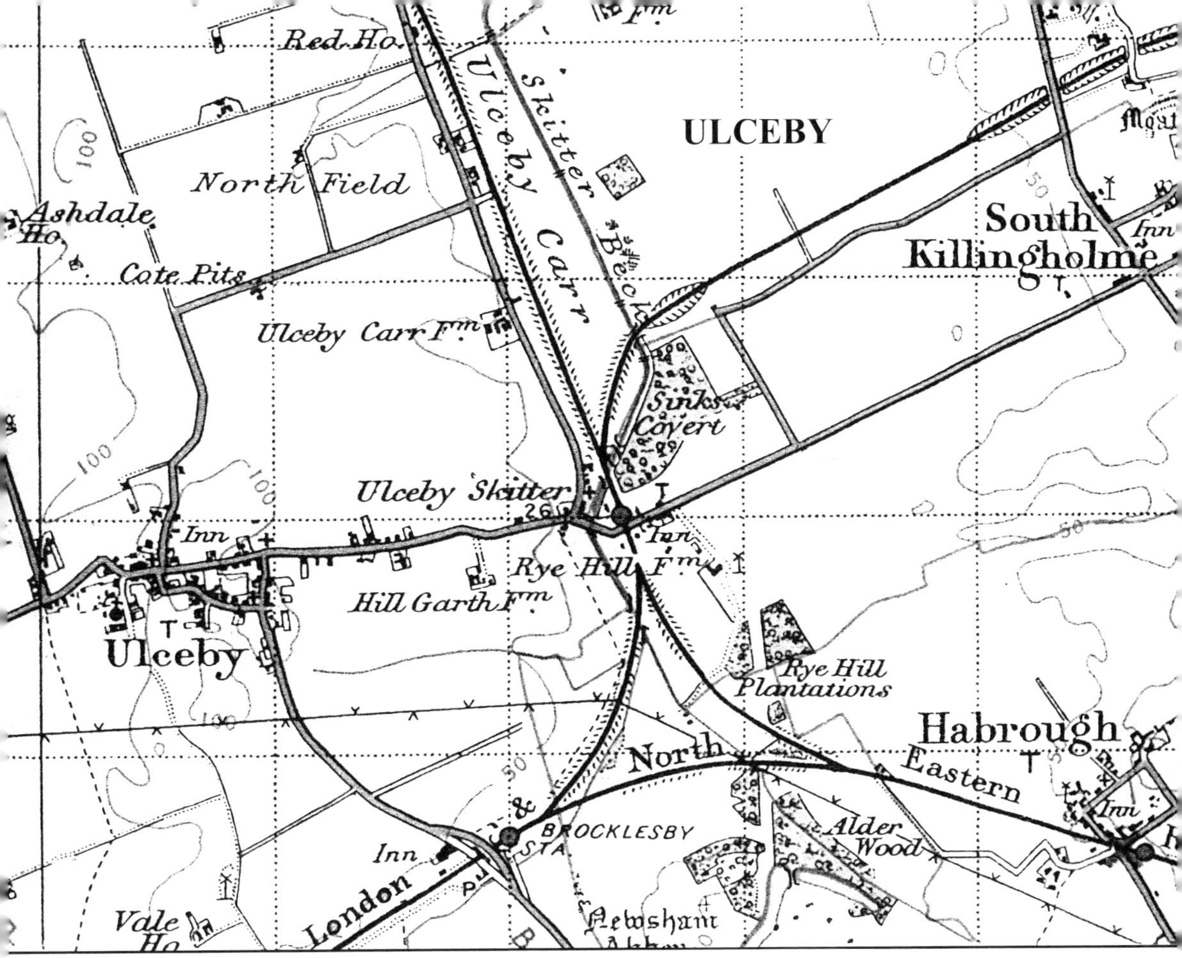

X. At 2ins to 1 mile is the 1947 survey. Our journey runs from the lower right to the top. Lower left is the line used by trains to Lincoln, Retford and Doncaster. Top right is the route to Immingham Dock. All lines were still in use in 2017, although trains to the latter were freight only.

28. We are looking north at an early postcard, with the signal box on the right. The village housed 865 in 1901 and 822 in 1961. In the early years, the express trains ran to New Holland and passengers for Grimsby had to change here. It was on a branch line. (P.Laming coll.)

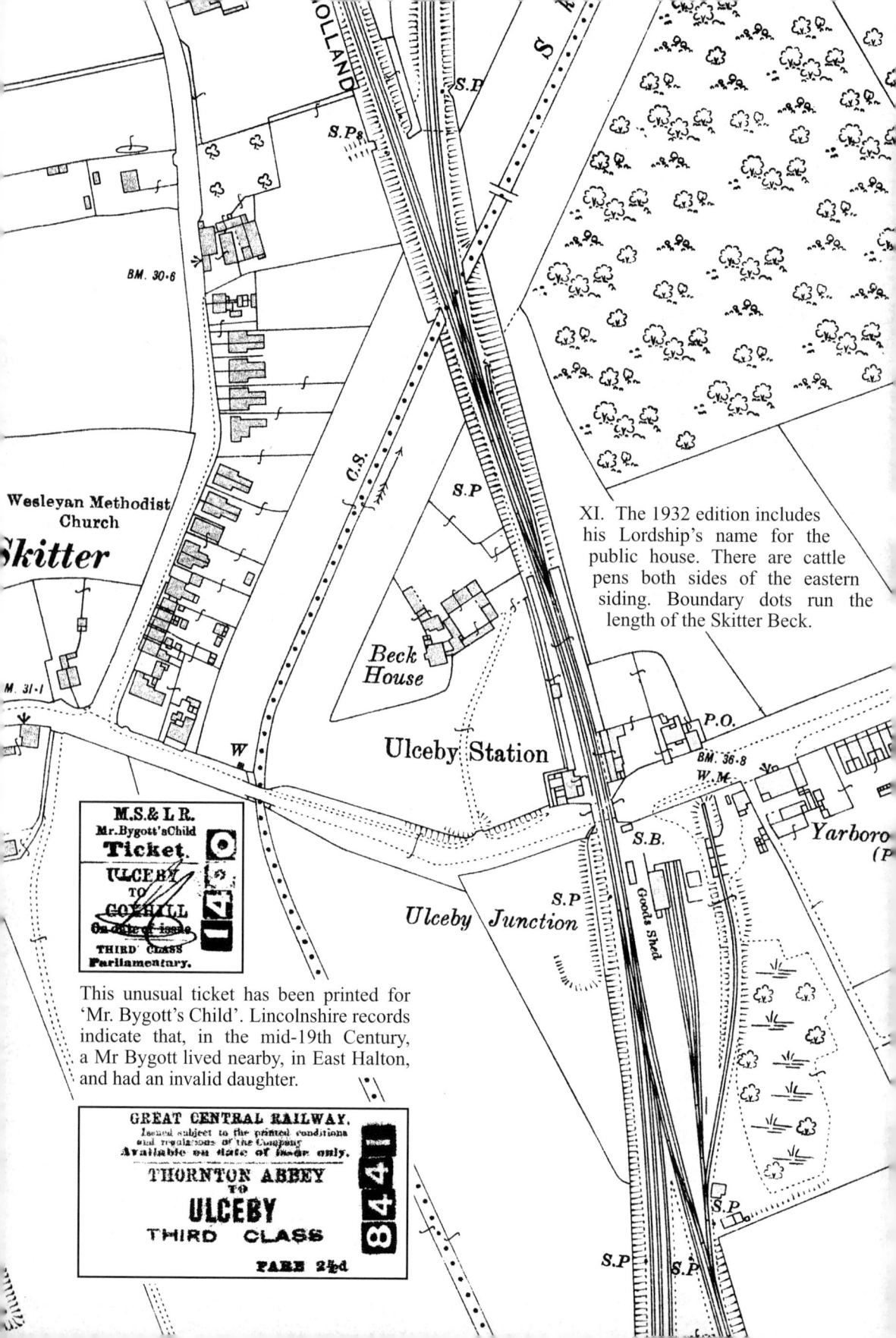

XI. The 1932 edition includes his Lordship's name for the public house. There are cattle pens both sides of the eastern siding. Boundary dots run the length of the Skitter Beck.

This unusual ticket has been printed for 'Mr. Bygott's Child'. Lincolnshire records indicate that, in the mid-19th Century, a Mr Bygott lived nearby, in East Halton, and had an invalid daughter.

29. A view in the other direction on another card completes the architectural coverage. In the background is part of the goods yard, which was in use until 16th June 1964. The 1910 signal box was in use until 30th December 2015 and worked the junction seen in picture 32. (P.Laming coll.)

30. Staffing of the station came to an end on 29th June 1969 and weather protection was lost at about that time. This is a sad scene when compared with picture 28. However, few stations showed junction signals in both directions. (R.Humm coll.)

31. A bridge arrived, but the level crossing was retained. The gates were replaced by half barriers in April 2007. The arrival of the A180 dual carriageway resulted in this bridge being removed. (J.Alsop coll.)

32. Three photographs from 27th July 1979 are from the new bridge just seen. This shows an oil train taking the curve to Immingham Dock and no. 47335 returning from there with a van. The platform on the left would soon be taken out of use, with all passengers using the other one, which was fit for two cars only. The left track was retained for freight traffic and the mobile steps were retired. (T.Heavyside)

33. A panorama in the other direction features the northern end of the triangular junction and a DMU from Cleethorpes, bound for New Holland. The box was opened in 1909, with a 60-lever frame. In 1988 this was reduced to 30 levers and a panel was added. The white tank was a recent addition. It contained gas for point heaters, which were in use until 1982. (T.Heavyside)

34. The box controlled the half-barriers from April 2007 and was demolished in January 2016. The station then had a two-hourly service in each direction on weekdays. It was operated by a class 153 railcar. The Sunday service was limited to the summer months only, with four trips each way. No. 47222 is hauling empty coal wagons to Immingham. (T.Heavyside)

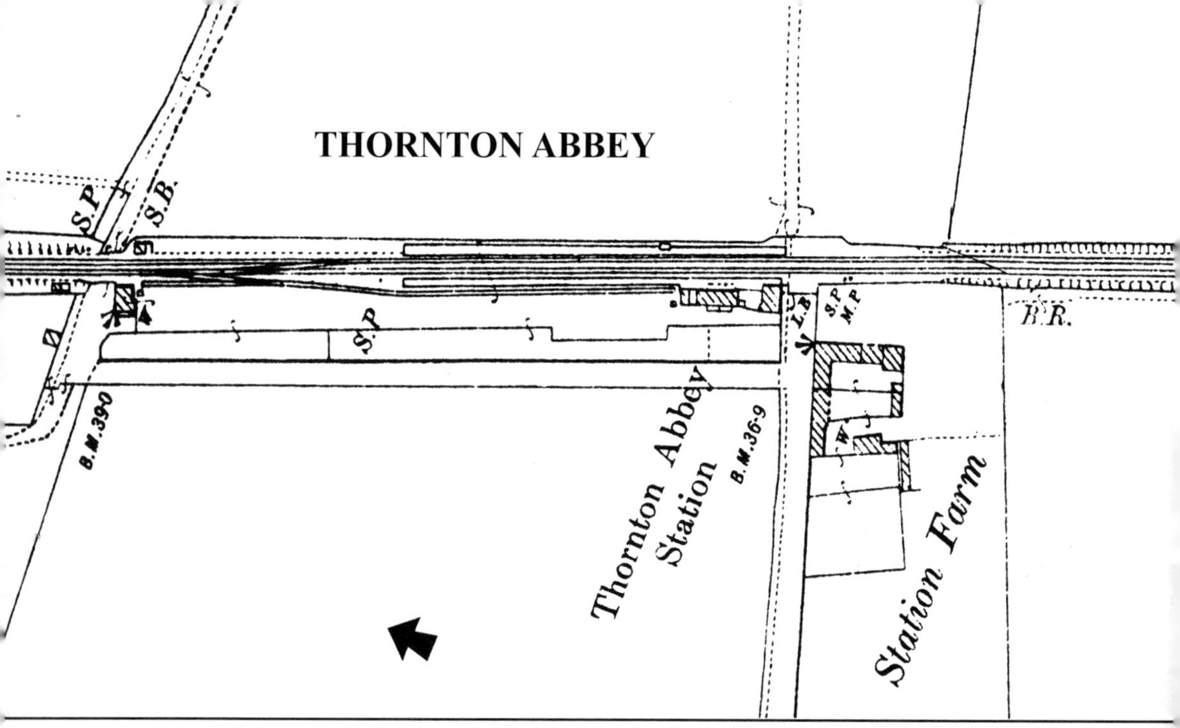

THORNTON ABBEY

XII. The 1906 edition shows the single siding and map II reveals the position of the village of Thornton Curtis, which the station served. The first station carried this name and was ½ mile to the south. It was in use between about April 1848 and August 1849. In the initial years, the Temperance Society's annual meetings here were attended by many thousands of members.

35. This northward view is from 28th April 1954 and includes the gate house at Barton Road. The gates were still manually worked in 2006 and further north there was Butterwood Crossing, which had automatic barriers. (H.C.Casserley)

36. A southward panorama in the 1960s looks towards the crossing at Bystable Lane, again manually worked. Both platforms could take three-car units in 2016 and, in 12 months, there were 1342 passengers. (LOSA)

37. Class 114 cars E53032 and E54016 call at a windswept-looking Thornton Abbey station with a New Holland-Cleethorpes train on 12th April 1983. Thornton Abbey had lost its goods facilities on 30th December 1963 and became an unstaffed halt on 29th June 1969. The old running-in boards survived nationalisation and in September 2009 they were renovated. The old metal letters were fitted to new boards by local enterprise groups. (P.D.Shannon)

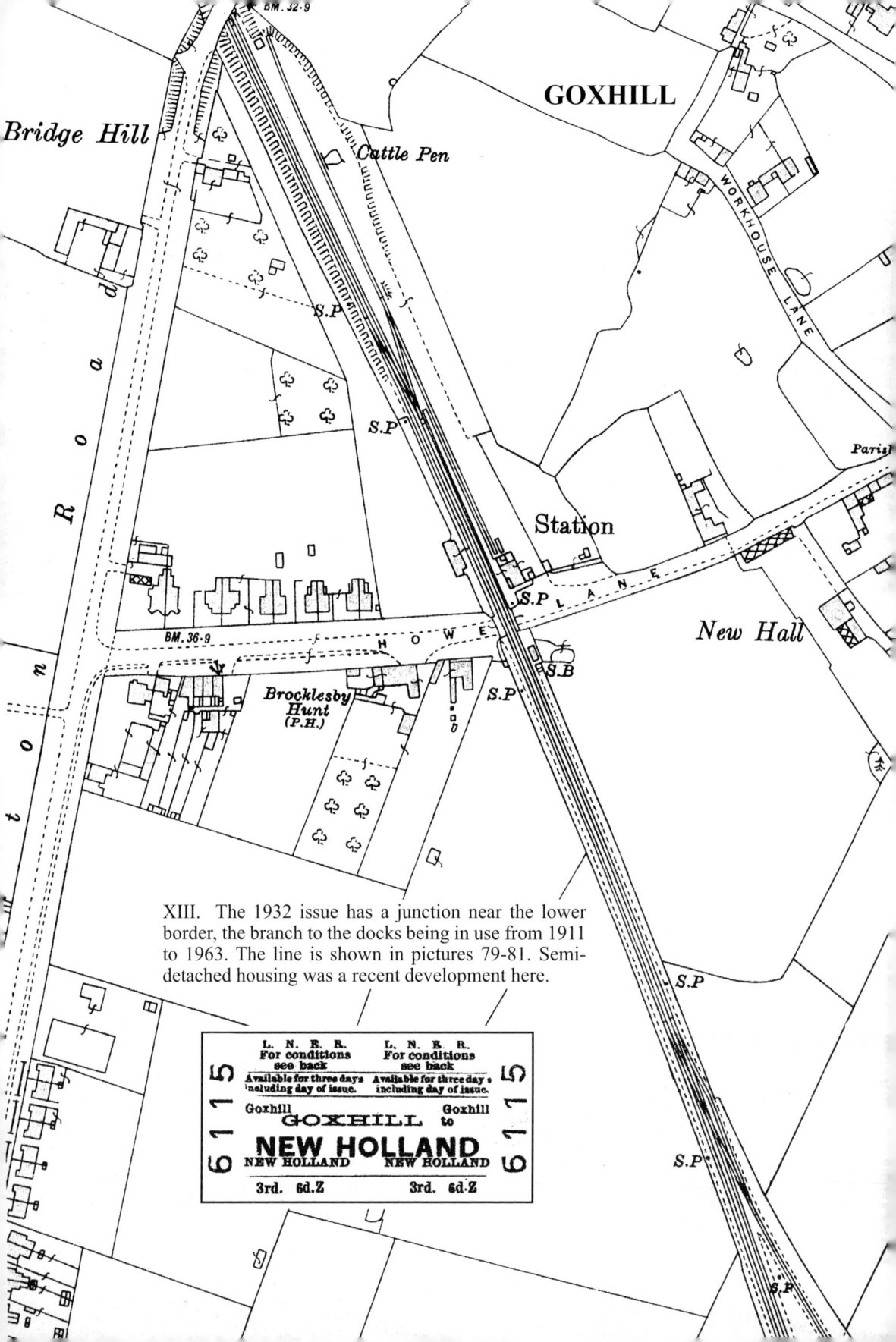

XIII. The 1932 issue has a junction near the lower border, the branch to the docks being in use from 1911 to 1963. The line is shown in pictures 79-81. Semi-detached housing was a recent development here.

38. A southward view includes the junction signals in the distance and the entrance gate to the goods yard on the left. Milk churns are on both platforms. (LOSA)

39. A closer look at the main building shows an unusual feature. On display is the mangle, presumably used by the wife of the station master to reduce washing water in clothes prior to hanging them up to dry. It is also unusual to see part of the gate wheel. (J.Alsop coll.)

40. Two photographs from 6th May 2017 show real impeccable conservation standards, plus gates still present. No. 153358 approaches, bound for Cleethorpes. It is the final station on the route northwards to have two platforms. (J.Whitehouse)

41. Both platforms were fit for four coaches and carried floral delights. The building was a private residence and the gates were moved by hand by the signaller. (J.Whitehouse)

SOUTH OF NEW HOLLAND

Oxmarsh Crossing

42. This location is shown lower right on the next map. No. 153301 is rounding the curve from Barrow Haven to enter the 1981 platform, on 13th May 1999. The overgrown siding on the right had served New Holland Bulk Services, where there were three parallel sidings. (M.Turvey)

Barrow Road Crossing

43. Barrow Road runs close to the gutter between the pages bearing the next map. The junction allowed freight traffic to continue straight to the dockside lines and passenger trains to diverge left to the curves to the station. (P.Laming coll.)

44. The course explained is best seen near the centre of the next map. The situation was recorded here on 13th May 2010. (R.Humm)

45. We move a little southwards on 10th August 2016 and rise onto the fresh platform provided in 1981, when the pier and its two 1848 stations closed. It is seen fully in picture no. 68. (R.Geach)

Engine Shed

46. This was a very busy shed from the outset, but as Grimsby grew, it steadily declined, during the 1880s in particular. Following the opening of Immingham Shed in 1912, it became a quiet sub-shed. It closed in 1938, when this photo was taken. (W.A.Camwell/R.Griffiths)

47. A view from June 1952 features ex-GCR 0-6-2T class N5 no. 69305. In its final years, the building served as a shelter for a single shunting engine, a Sentinel and, later, a diesel. The coaling stage was beyond the left section and the water tank is on the right. (R.S.Carpenter coll.)

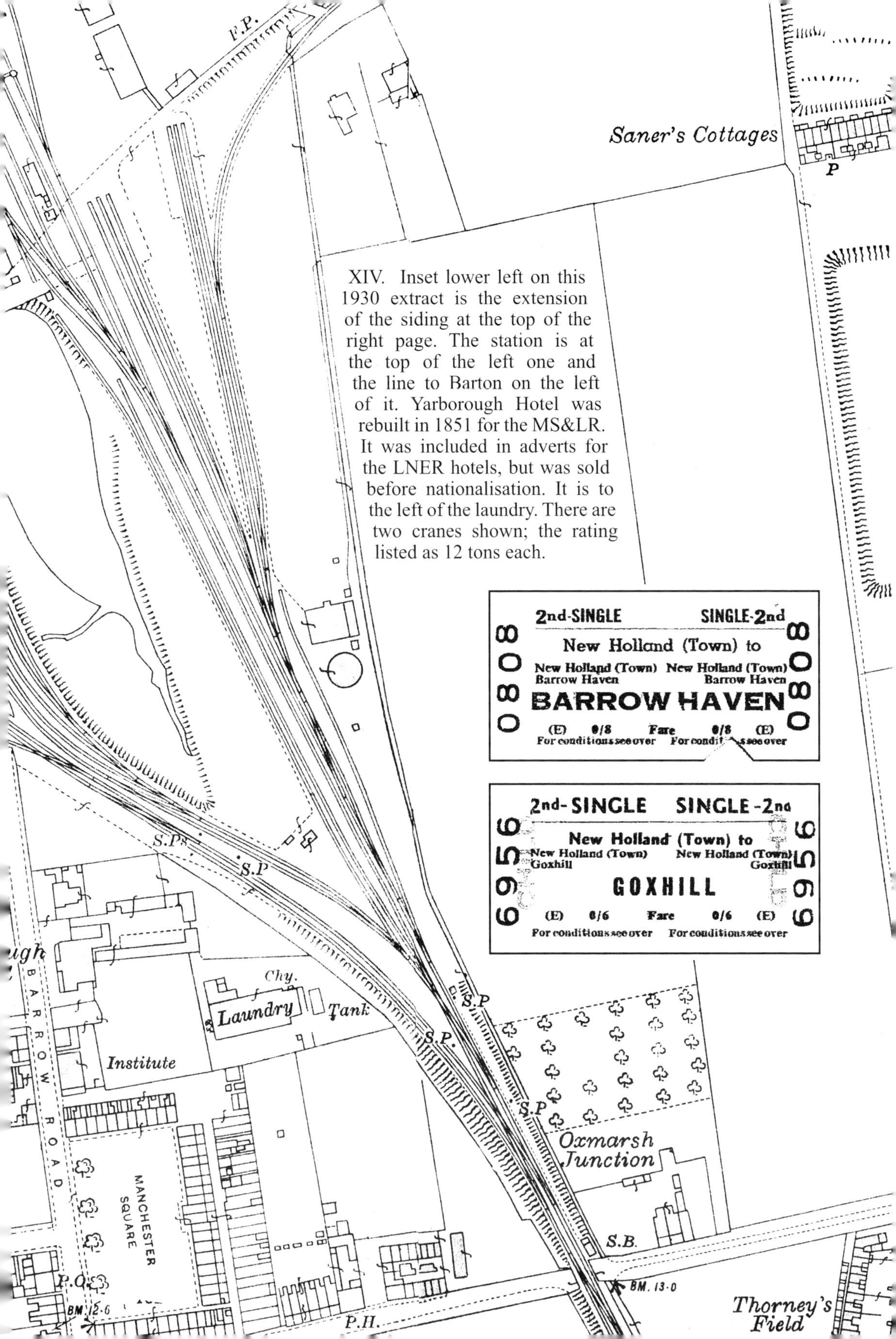

XIV. Inset lower left on this 1930 extract is the extension of the siding at the top of the right page. The station is at the top of the left one and the line to Barton on the left of it. Yarborough Hotel was rebuilt in 1851 for the MS&LR. It was included in adverts for the LNER hotels, but was sold before nationalisation. It is to the left of the laundry. There are two cranes shown; the rating listed as 12 tons each.

48. We gaze towards the pier from the crossing in front of the signal box. The merit of the later introduction of the short word CAFÉ from France becomes clear. (LOSA)

49. We are looking north from the apex of the triangle on the left page on map XIV. The signal box is to the right of the engine and one siding curves behind it. (LOSA)

50. Running in with a train from Cleethorpes on 14th April 1947 is class B3 4-6-0 no. 1496. Its name was *Valour* and it was withdrawn in November 1947. The Barton-on-Humber lines are on the right and the two carriage sidings are on the left. (H.C.Casserley)

51. Seen on 28th April 1954 is class 0-6-2T no. 69305 waiting with the 2.5pm departure to Barton-on-Humber. The word TOWN was used to a limited extent; not helpful to strangers. (H.C.Casserley)

52. The disused main entrance was recorded on 6th July 1976, the year of the heatwave. This is the east elevation. The map shows that there had been a siding in the foreground in earlier days. (R.Humm)

53. The crossing was at the north end of Barrow Road and carried no through traffic. This explains why there were only two gates and short ones at that. They appear to have been wheel driven. (LOSA)

54. The pier decking starts in the foreground of this 1979 panorama. The barrier on the right indicates that only short trains were running two years before pier closure. Goods traffic ceased on 3rd November 1979. (R.Humm coll.)

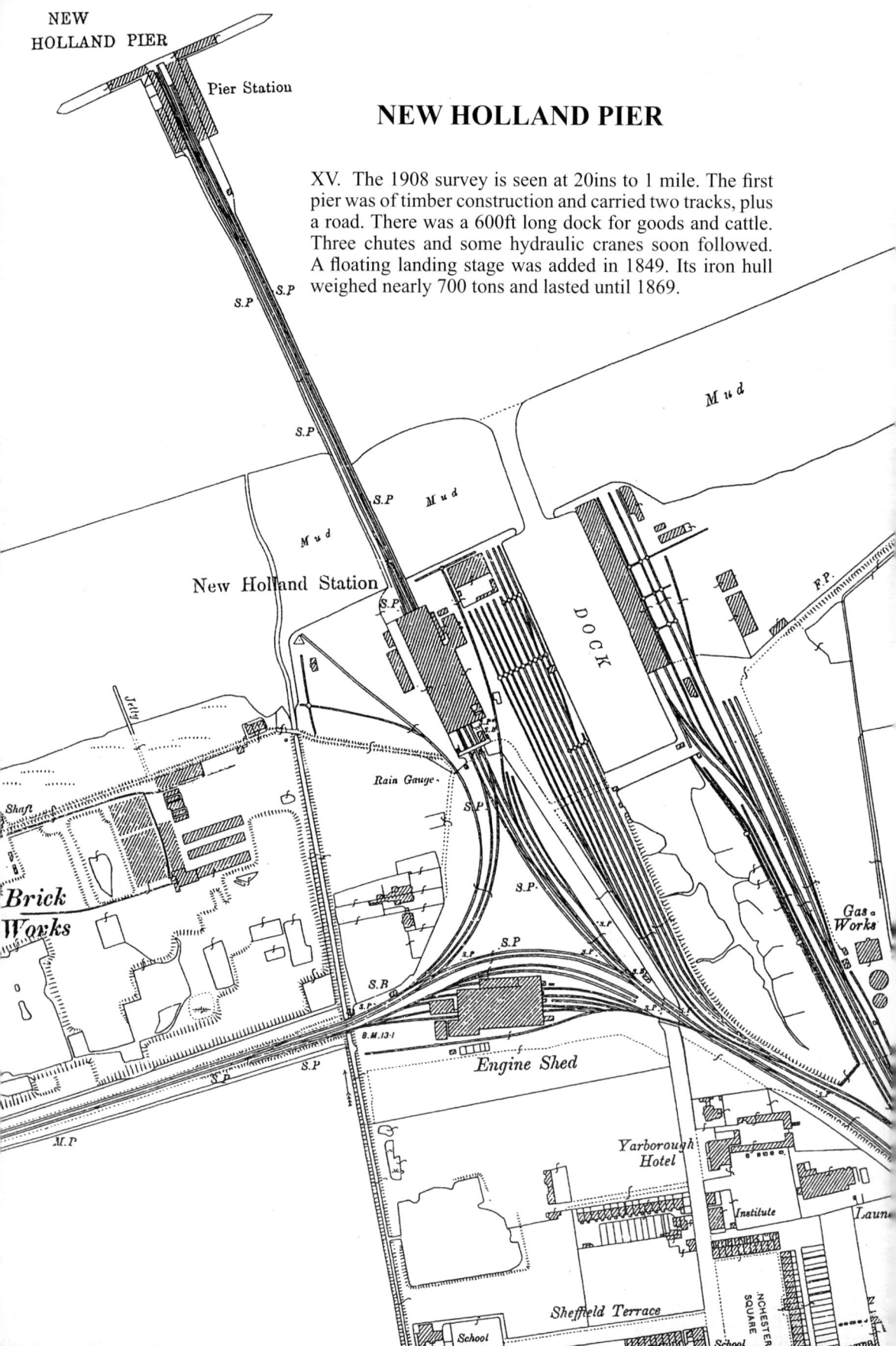

NEW HOLLAND PIER

XV. The 1908 survey is seen at 20ins to 1 mile. The first pier was of timber construction and carried two tracks, plus a road. There was a 600ft long dock for goods and cattle. Three chutes and some hydraulic cranes soon followed. A floating landing stage was added in 1849. Its iron hull weighed nearly 700 tons and lasted until 1869.

55. This is one of several paddle steamers operated by the MS&LR between the pier and Hull. By 1842, there were about 25 ferries working in the estuary. (A.Dudman coll.)

56. The map shows that an overall roof was provided initially on the Town station, but not here. This 2-4-0 was in use from 1873 to 1916. (LOSA)

57. The pier was rebuilt in 1928, but details have not been published. This appears to be 4-4-0 no. N360. It must be pre-1923, as LNER distant signals did not carry bars. (J.Alsop coll.)

58. This is the Pier Head in about 1920. The buildings included refreshment rooms and conveniences. The inclined deck could accept ferries at different heights of tide. (R.Humm coll.)

59. *Tattershall Castle* has cast off for Hull on 10th May 1946. It is in the distance. The ship had a three-cylinder steam engine and was built in 1934, in Hartlepool. It is carrying two road vehicles. This ship retired to London's Embankment to offer refreshments. *Wingfield Castle* could later be found at Hartlepool and *Lincoln Castle* at Hessle, across the water. (H.C.Casserley)

60. The centre road was used as a run-round for engines and its northern end often contained wagons of coal needed by the ferries. The 1.52pm to Cleethorpes on 10th May 1946 is behind class C4 4-4-2 no. 6083. (H.C.Casserley)

61. Waiting to leave at 7.40pm for Cleethorpes on 9th June 1947 is no. 2909, a class C4. On the left is the 7.47 to Barton, which is hauled by no. 9322, a class N5. (W.A.Camwell/SLS)

62. The 9.58am to Cleethorpes on 27th April 1954 was hauled by no. 61142, a class B1 4-6-0, rated as 5MT. The design was introduced by the LNER in 1942 and 409 were listed in 1961. (R.M.Casserley)

63. A panorama from the next day includes no. 69305 with the 2.05pm to Barton-on-Humber and no. 69820 leaving with the 1.45pm to Immingham Dock. This was a class A5 4-6-2T. (H.C.Casserley)

64. P.S. *Lincoln Castle* was completed for the LNER in 1940 and was photographed on 5th May 1960. One of the paddles is concealed between the two access points. The gross tonnage was 598, it carried a crew of 12 and up to 1200 passengers. By the time of the station's closure, the service was operated solely by Sealink's *Farringford*, a diesel-powered paddle ferry dating from 1947. (P.J.Kelley)

65. The platform on the left was linked to the station on the coast and was used by motor cars being conveyed by a ferry. The Hull coastline is evident as a DMU waits to leave for Cleethorpes.
(D.K.Jones coll.)

66. It is 29th March 1970 and coal wagons wait to fuel the ferry boilers. The buildings became very shabby in the final years. The 16.45 waits to leave, all stations to Cleethorpes, and a Morris 1100 car departs for land.
(SLS coll.)

67. It is 29th October 1980 and we can enjoy our final view from the pier and glimpse at the 'straight & narrow' for cars. The pier reopened in 1998 for grain and animal feed, the buildings being renovated for this new purpose. The signal box was retained, complete with its frame. By 1999, a Sentinel 0-6-0 diesel was the pilot engine here. (D.K.Jones coll.)

NEW HOLLAND

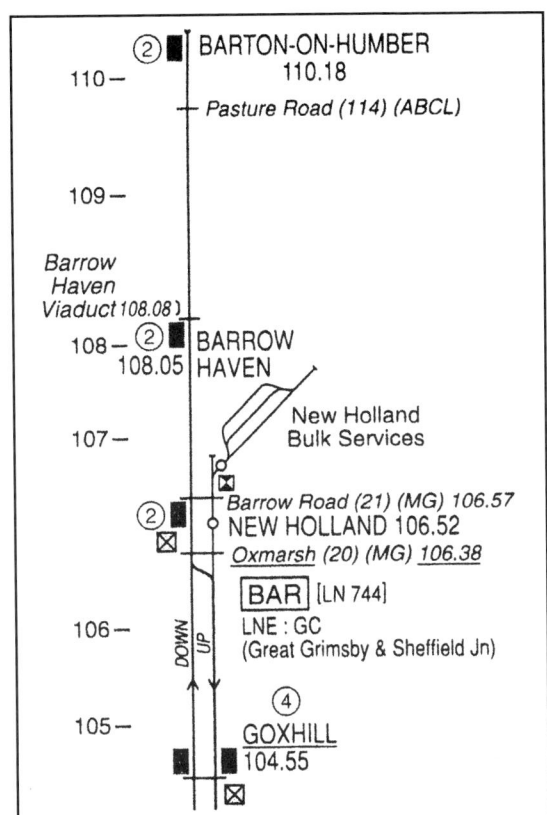

XVI. This is the layout in 2010. It is diagrammatic, not geographic.
(© TRACKmaps)

68. We return to the location shown in picture 45 to see fully the platform brought into use on 25th June 1981 to replace the locations found in pictures 48 to here. This view is from 26th October 1981 and includes Barrow Road level crossing. (D.A.Thompson)

BARROW HAVEN

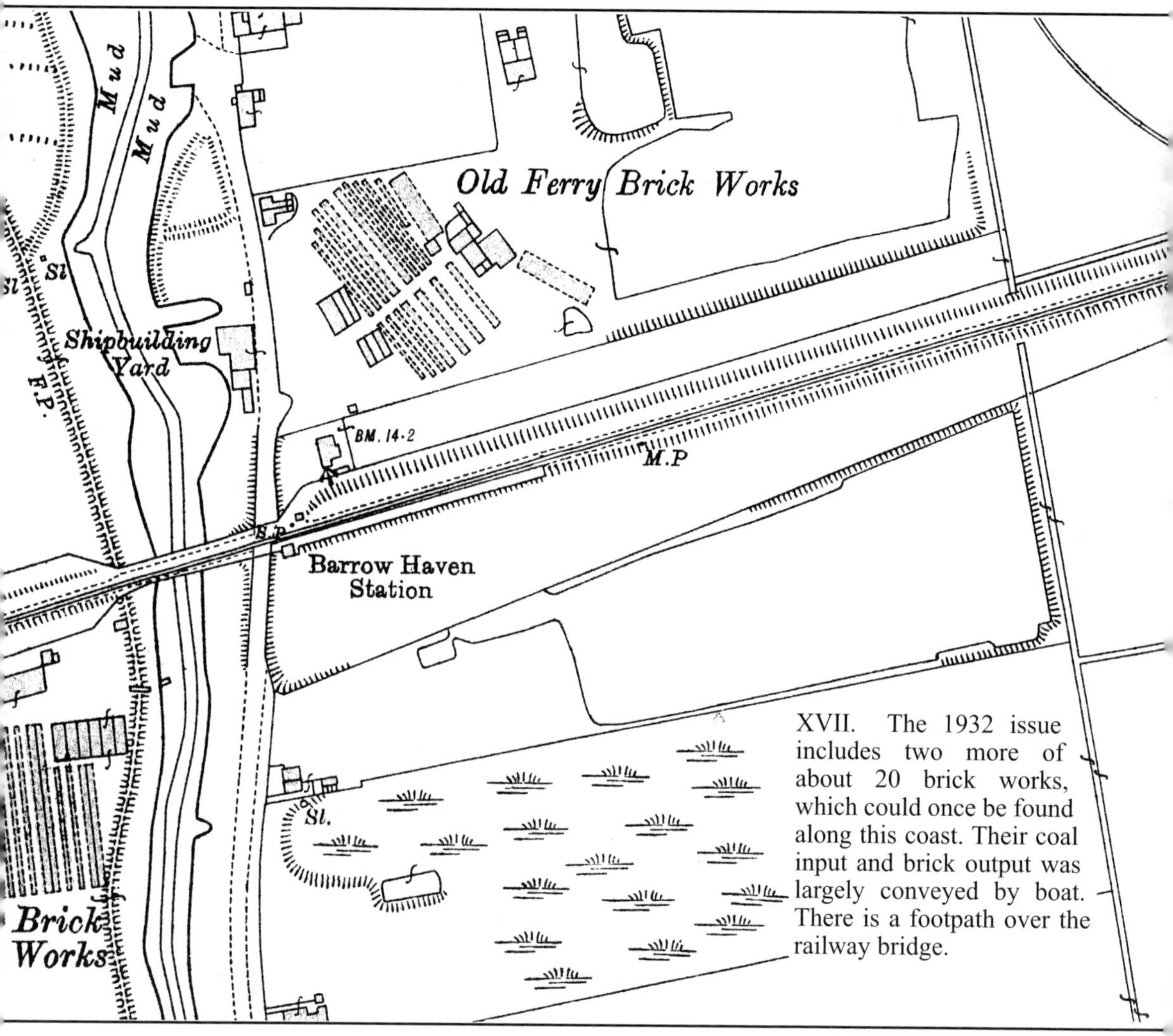

XVII. The 1932 issue includes two more of about 20 brick works, which could once be found along this coast. Their coal input and brick output was largely conveyed by boat. There is a footpath over the railway bridge.

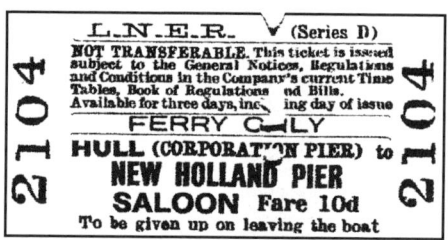

69. Only a booking hall is on offer in this undated view. A tiny garden and white-washed trimmings enhanced the scene. By 1980, the station had become an unofficial bird observatory; a neatly-typed bulletin in the booking office window listed sightings from the station of rare birds, such as Ruffs and Manx Shearwaters. Barrow Haven brickyard still had some of its 2ft gauge line in use. (J.Alsop coll.)

70. The minimal provision was recorded on 8th May 1999, as Sprinter no. 153351 called. These cars were converted from 2-car class 155s in 1991-92. Annual passengers numbered around 1600 in 2015-16. (M.Turvey)

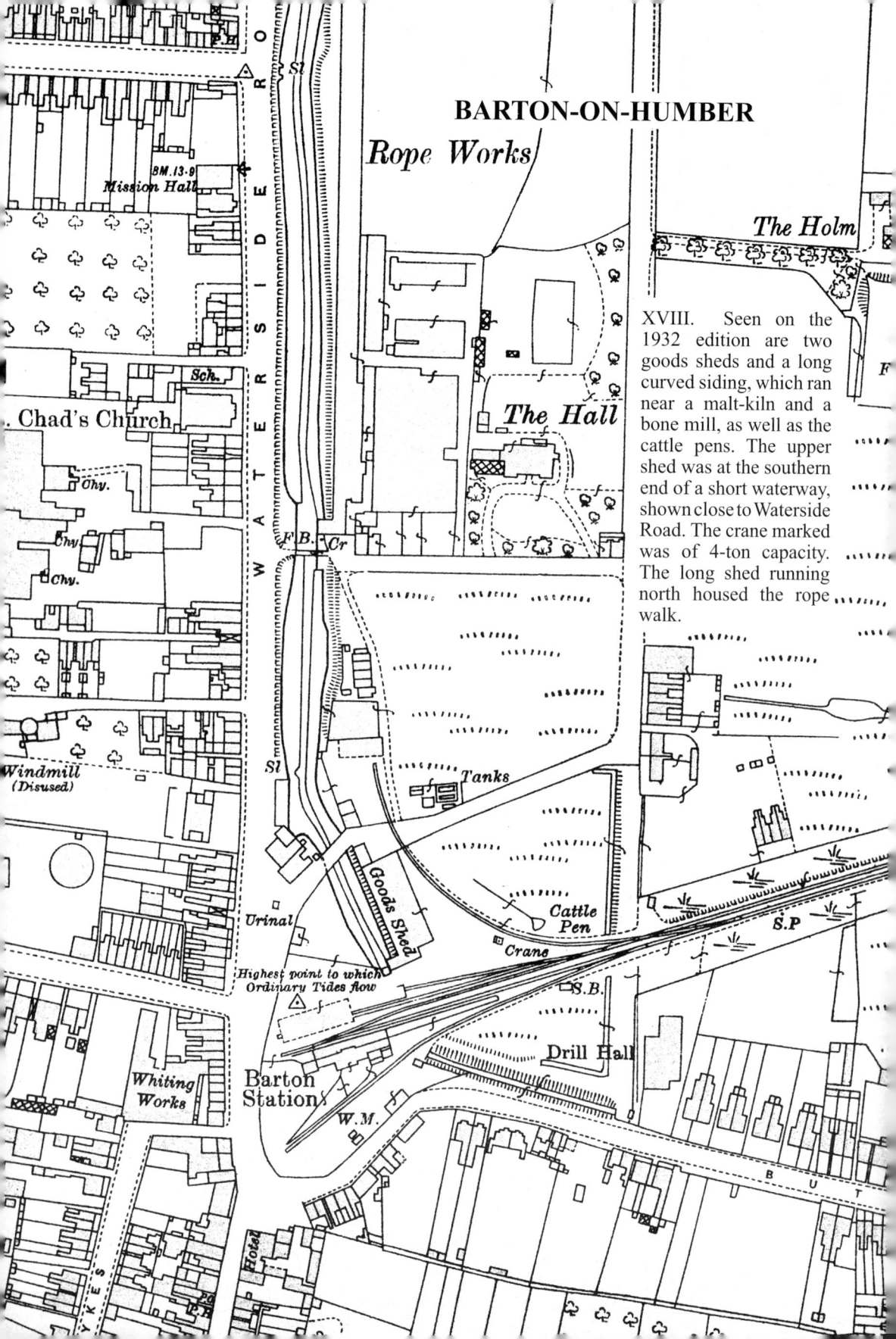

XVIII. Seen on the 1932 edition are two goods sheds and a long curved siding, which ran near a malt-kiln and a bone mill, as well as the cattle pens. The upper shed was at the southern end of a short waterway, shown close to Waterside Road. The crane marked was of 4-ton capacity. The long shed running north housed the rope walk.

71. The GCR moved one of its steam railmotors here to work the branch in the early years of the 20th Century. They were fitted with vertical boilers. One is illustrated in picture 106. The booking office window is under the short unsupported roof. A horse nods as a bicycle is manhandled; novel features for a postcard. On the left are the western points of the loop. (LOSA)

72. A view from April 1947 reveals an unexpected number of trollies; presumably they served peak demands. The siding on the left had run to coal drops in the previous century. (H.C.Casserley)

73. There was a private siding about one mile to the east to the chemical works of Albright & Wilson until 1988. Train loads of phosphoric acid came to it from Cumbria. The south elevation was photographed on 28th April 1954. (H.C.Casserley)

74. The crew rest on the same day, as does no. 69305, a class N5 0-6-2T. The population grew from 5671 in 1901 to 6590 in 1961, reaching 11,006 by 2011. (H.C.Casserley)

75. DMUs were seen regularly from 1956 displaying 'Cats Whiskers', as shown here on 23rd July 1961. The goods shed can be seen to be totally devoid of security. Its traffic ceased on 3rd August 1970 and the yard on the left also closed. (E.Wilmshurst)

76. Staffing of the station ceased on 29th June 1969 and the short roof was removed. The loading gauge remained for a time. All the buildings were demolished in 1973. (LOSA)

77. It is 1st February 1986 and class 101 nos 53207 and 54088 will shortly depart at 12.00 to Grimsby. A bus station was built nearby, so that one could cross the Humber every 30 minutes during the day. The service ran between Hull and Scunthorpe. (A.C.Hartless)

78. On 8th May 1999, no. 153351 was working the 15.50 to Cleethorpes. This platform was built in 1998 on a fresh alignment. (M.Turvey)

2. Barton & Immingham Light Railway

EAST HALTON HALT

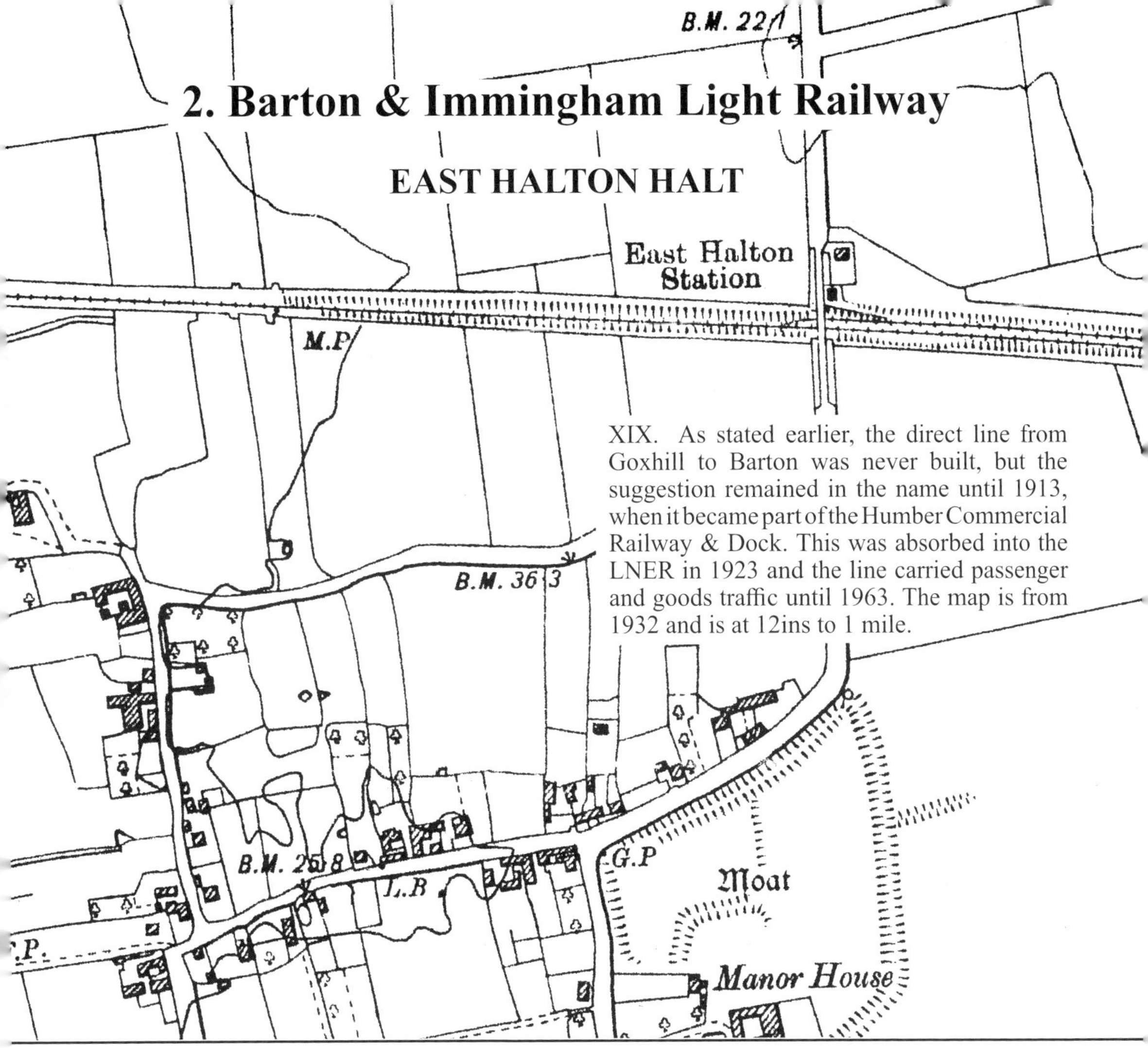

XIX. As stated earlier, the direct line from Goxhill to Barton was never built, but the suggestion remained in the name until 1913, when it became part of the Humber Commercial Railway & Dock. This was absorbed into the LNER in 1923 and the line carried passenger and goods traffic until 1963. The map is from 1932 and is at 12ins to 1 mile.

79. The hut at the top of the path housed the ticket office until staffing ceased on 2nd August 1948 and the term HALT was added to the name. This picture is thus before that time. (LOSA)

80. We are looking towards the Dock in this snap from 28th April 1953. Only small fires could be considered, as just one bucket remained. There was economy on the seat, as HALT had been painted on. (R.M.Casserley)

KILLINGHOLME

Admiralty Platform

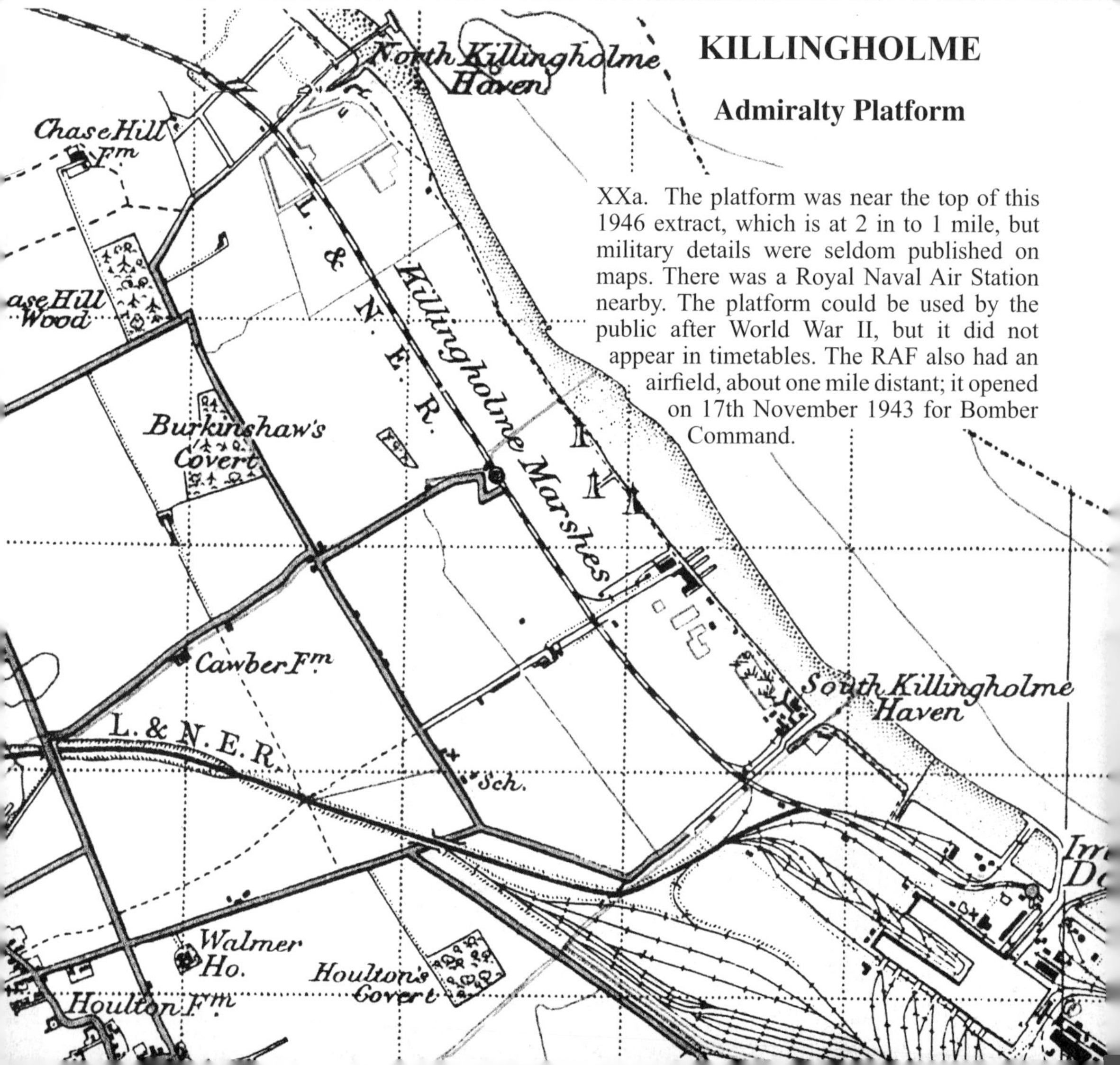

XXa. The platform was near the top of this 1946 extract, which is at 2 in to 1 mile, but military details were seldom published on maps. There was a Royal Naval Air Station nearby. The platform could be used by the public after World War II, but it did not appear in timetables. The RAF also had an airfield, about one mile distant; it opened on 17th November 1943 for Bomber Command.

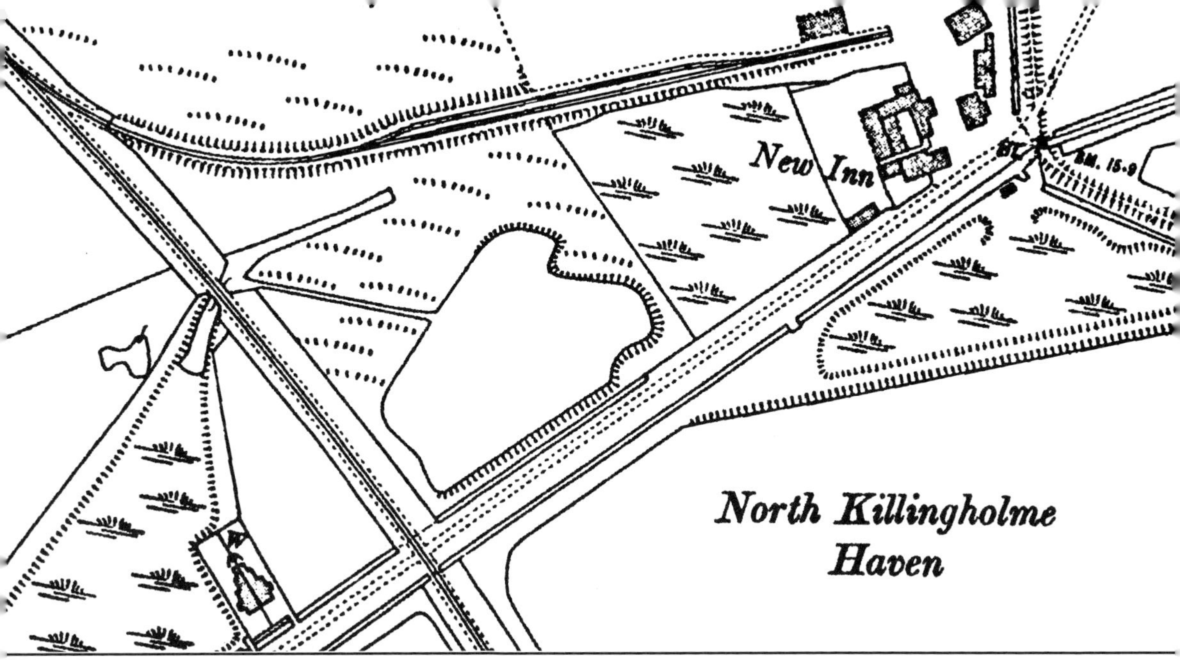

North Killingholme
Haven

XXb. The 1930 survey reveals a siding, but its purpose has not been established with certainty. Naval traffic was likely.

81a. The view towards the Dock was recorded on 28th April 1954. HALT was applied on 1st September 1955. Closure came on 17th June 1963. It had come into use on 17th March 1913 to serve a Naval vessel refuelling base called North Killingholme. Oil tankers can be seen in the background. The US Navy had seaplanes based here in 1918. (H.C.Casserley)

Killingholme Halt

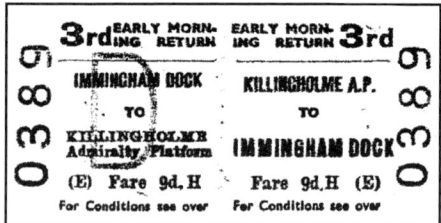

XXc. The 1930 edition refers to a station; it also became a halt on 1st September 1955. The goods yard was in use until 4th January 1965.

81b. Passengers were carried from 5th December 1910 until 17th June 1963, when the route closed. However, the track was still usable south of here and it can be found top left on diagram XXII. The RCTS railtour on 7th October 1967 reversed here and is seen with its class 114 DMU. It ran from and back to Barnetby and toured the dock lines.
(RCTS Archive)

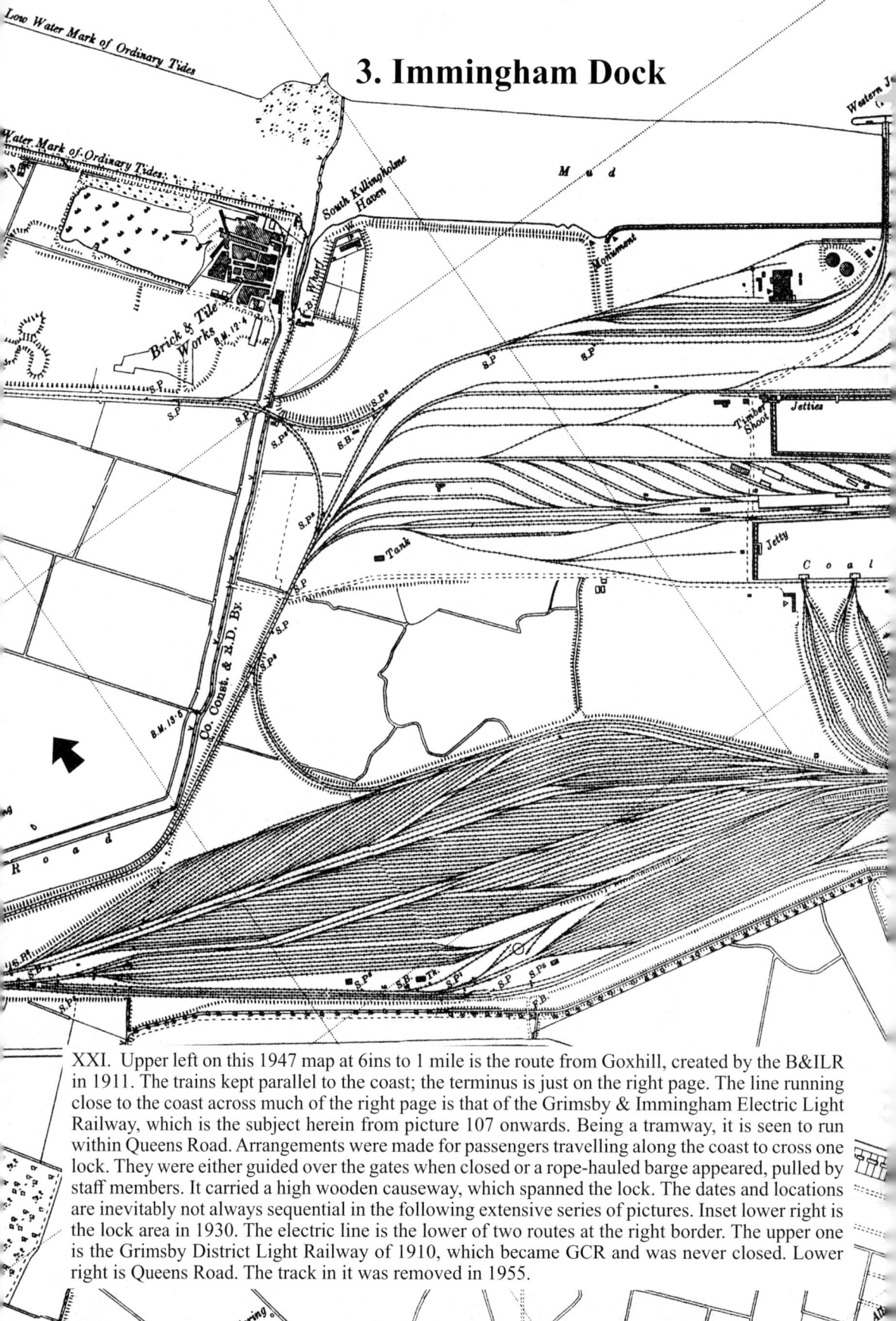

3. Immingham Dock

XXI. Upper left on this 1947 map at 6ins to 1 mile is the route from Goxhill, created by the B&ILR in 1911. The trains kept parallel to the coast; the terminus is just on the right page. The line running close to the coast across much of the right page is that of the Grimsby & Immingham Electric Light Railway, which is the subject herein from picture 107 onwards. Being a tramway, it is seen to run within Queens Road. Arrangements were made for passengers travelling along the coast to cross one lock. They were either guided over the gates when closed or a rope-hauled barge appeared, pulled by staff members. It carried a high wooden causeway, which spanned the lock. The dates and locations are inevitably not always sequential in the following extensive series of pictures. Inset lower right is the lock area in 1930. The electric line is the lower of two routes at the right border. The upper one is the Grimsby District Light Railway of 1910, which became GCR and was never closed. Lower right is Queens Road. The track in it was removed in 1955.

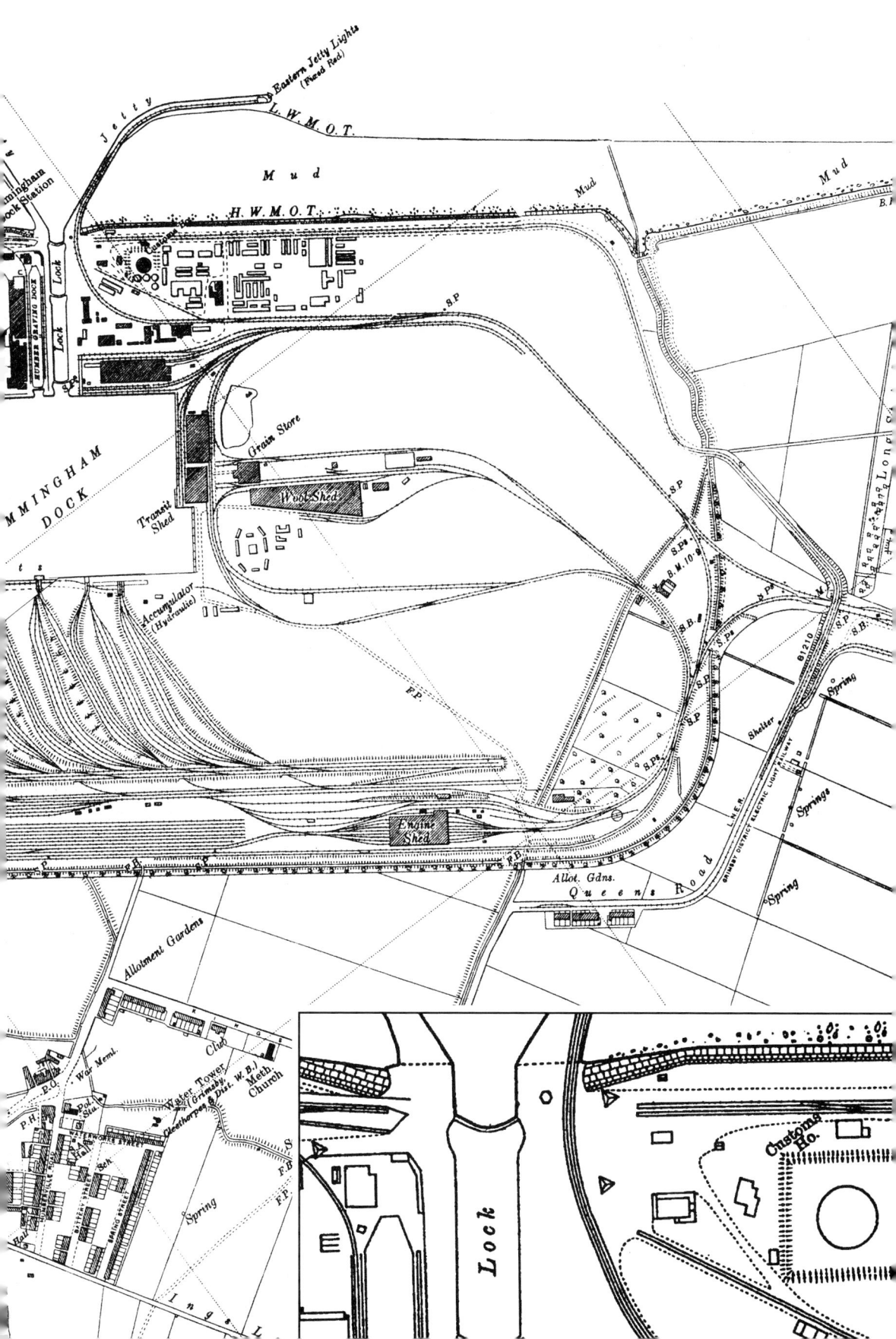

IMMINGHAM BULK TERMINAL
WESTERN JETTY
EASTERN JETTY
North Killingholme Cargo Terminal (Simon Storage)
Admiralty Sdgs EWS
Killingholme EWS
Marsh Farm (5) (open) 0.49
Humber International Terminal APB
APB Cabin
[LN 742]
2 KIL 1
COM
0.00 | 5.10
(Humber Rd LC)
✱ = Simon Storage West (TMO)
Simon Storage West
INW
105.16
Western Storage
Dock Tank Farm
North Western Entrance
107.32
Simon Storage (Texaco)
ENGINEERS SDG (ESSO BAY)
Simon Storage (open)
No. 1 Quay
Transit
600 Series S
Bunkers 1 & 2
WB
NR Bdy 0.06
KILLINGHOLME DOWN
UP
2.39
Yorkshire Tar (20) (TMO) 2.44
Shell Mex (19) (open) 2.34
New Inn (18) (open) 2.19
[LN 742]
KIL 2
LNE : GC
(Barton & Immingham Light)
No. 2 ARR/DEP
No. 1 ARR/DEP
0.11
0.06
0.02
COAL PAD 2 LINE
COAL PAD 1 LINE
ORE LINE
Overhead Conveyor
(IW)
104.79
Immingham West Jn
104.78
104.77
HENDERSON QUAY
Mineral Quay Sdgs
RR LOOP
Seawheel Sdgs
TRANSIT QUAYS
Astra Fuels
No. 2 & 3 Qua
SHED SIDE
MIDDLE ROAD
DOCK SIDE
Loading Bunker
MINERAL QUAY (EXXTOR)
STORA ENSO
104.67
104.72
Western Entrance (CCTV) 104.55
Mineral Quay (TMO)
Immingham Bulk Terminal Corus
IMMINGHAM DOCK
Associated British Ports (NCBO)
IMMINGHAM Lindsey Refinery
Total & Petrofina
Arrival Sdgs North
RELEASE
Departure Sidings
Loading Sidings
Gantry
Coal Export Terminal
Coal Products Ltd
'A' Sorting Sgs
ABP
'Astra'
'Hargreaves Fuels'
EXXTOR
Immingham C&W EWS
'B' Sorting Sidings
Discharge Area
old CW Sidings
WORKSHOP RD
Rotary Tippler Servicing Shed
COAL ROAD
DEAD END
MAINTENANCE
Nordic
LC
UP KILLINGHOLME
DOWN KILLINGHOLME
Bunker
[LN 742]
KIL 1
UP MAIN
DOWN MAIN
Dock Boundary
105
Arrival Sdgs South
Control Tower
Controlled by (IR)
Marcroft
Reception Sidings : EWS
WB
104
(Dock Bdy)
104.08
SHUNT SPUR
(IR)
EMPTY
SIDINGS LINE
UP MAIN 103.19
DOWN MAIN
WEST CURVE
EAST CURVE
103.54
103.45
Immingham Gate
104.05 Humber Rd Jn
Immingham Reception Sidings 104.30
Ambulance (15) (UWC) 104.39
[LN 740]
BRI 2
LNE : GC
(Humber Coal Rly. & Dock)
Miles from Manchester (London Road) via Woodhead
Storage
Gantry
LS
Loading Sdgs
IMMINGHAM : Humber Refinery
Conoco

L. N. E. R.
FOR CONDITIONS SEE BACK. Available for three days including day of issue.
KILLINGHOLME to
KILLINGHOLME (ADMIRALTY PLATFORM)
3691
Fare
THIRD
S 2110
3½d.P
CLASS

3rd - SINGLE SINGLE - 3rd
IMMINGHAM DOCK to
Immingham Dock Immingham Dock
BARTON-ON-H. BARTON-ON-H.
BARTON-ON-HUMBER
Via Goxhill
(E) 2/1 H Fare 2/1 H (E)
For Conditions see over For Conditions see over
2516

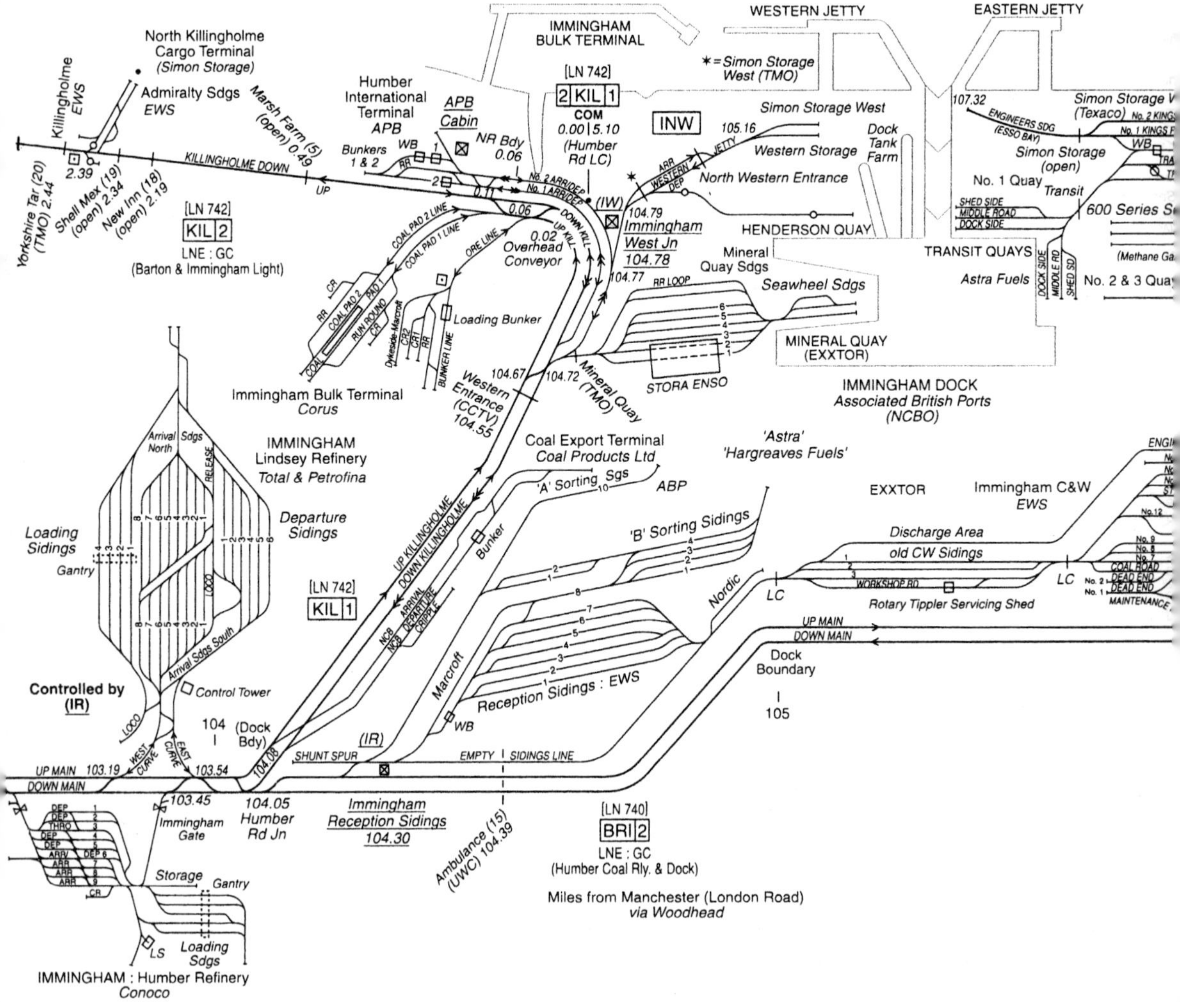

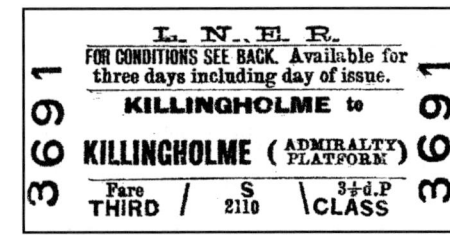

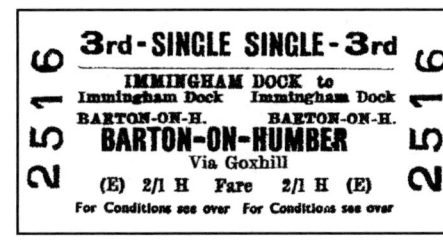

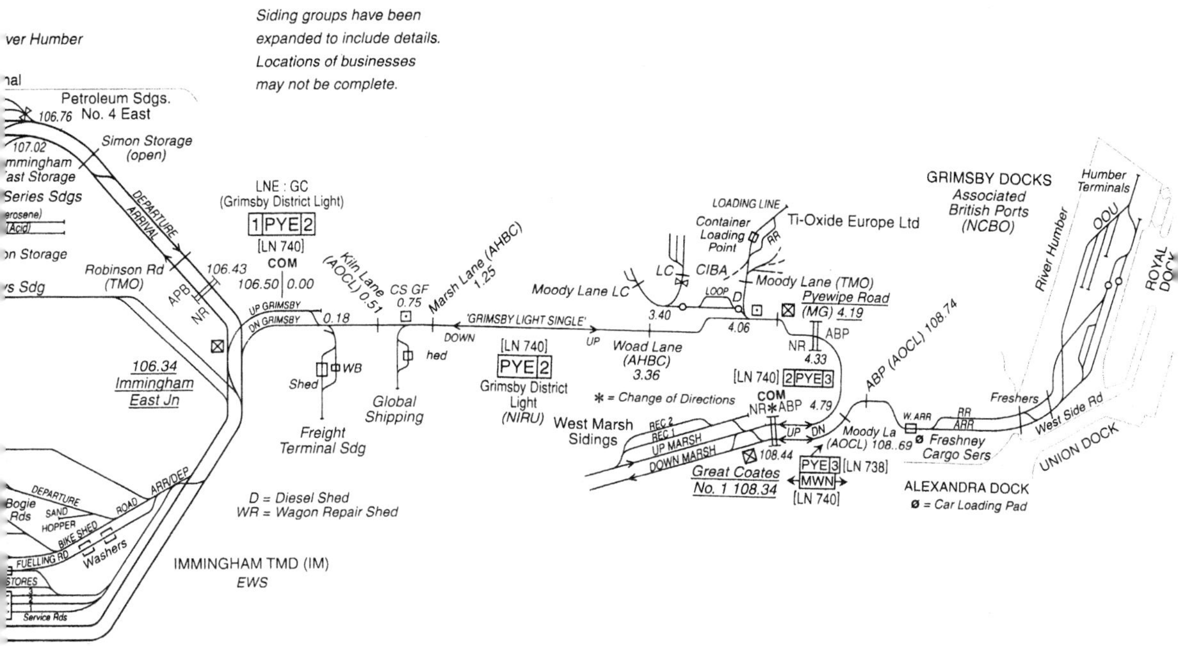

XXII. The complex layout was recorded in September 2006. The double track lower left is from Ulceby (picture 32) and the pair lower centre on the right page link with Marsh Junction (map V, lower left). On the right of this page are the Western Docks at Grimsby. Squares containing X indicate a signal box. Not shown here were 'Empty Sidings', which had a 76-lever frame signal box from 1912 until 1971. Pyewipe Road Box is shown. It had 20 levers, but most were unused. Great Coates No. 1 is nearby; it had 23 levers and was still open in 2016. No. 2 had 70 and was in use in 1909-66. Fisons had sidings here from 1950. The former Admiralty Sidings are marked top left. Many oil and chemical firms came in the 1950s. Several pipelines followed. (© TRACKmaps)

BRITISH RLYS. (E) BRITISH RLYS. (E)
For conditions see back For conditions see back
Available for three days including day of issue Available for three days including day of issue
3456 Immingham Dock Immingham Dock 3456
IMMINGHAM DOCK to
GOXHILL
GOXHILL GOXHILL
3rd. 1s.7d.Z 3rd. 1s.7d.Z

3rd - SINGLE SINGLE - 3rd
6673 IMMINGHAM DOCK TO 6673
Immingham Dock Killingholme (A.P.) Immingham Dock Killingholme (A.P.)
KILLINGHOLME
(ADMIRALTY PLATFORM)
(E) 0/7 Fare 0/7 (E)
For conditions see over For conditions see over

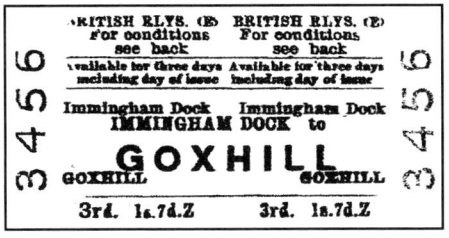

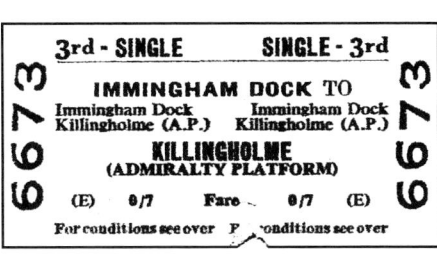

Immingham Dock station

82. In this postcard view, we look west with the terminus on the right. One of the light houses and the route to Western Jetty are the other important features in the view. The big chimney serves the electric and hydraulic power stations. (J.Alsop coll.)

83. LNER 4-4-0 class D7 no. 5683 has just arrived and is being coaled up, some time in the 1930s. This class was widely used in the district. There is a guards lookout at both ends of the train, the coaches of which have six wheels each. (R.Humm coll.)

↓ 84. No. 69820 is in a shabby condition in about 1950, as it waits upon arrival, attached to a semi-retired main line clerestory coach. It is a class A5 4-6-2T. The van at the rear would have been for extra luggage or mail traffic. (SLS coll.)

85. The same locomotive was recorded in better condition on 28th April 1954, waiting with the 12.10pm to New Holland. The terminus of the electric railway is in the background, but the locks are below ground level. There was an unadvertised train for workmen between here and Cleethorpes, in the mid-1950s. (R.M.Casserley)

86. This DMU is waiting to depart on 16th September 1961, in the days of rear lamps and observation saloons at no cost. The body styling was known as 'Cats Whiskers'. After completion, the Dock had 166 miles of track. (E.Wilmshurst)

87. Fisons Wharf was photographed in 1957. Rails for trains are between the outer ones, which are for the cranes. A 50-ton capacity crane was listed in 1938. (R.Humm coll.)

Western Jetty

88. We are looking north across the mud to the deeper water beyond the jetty, which carried the railway tracks on the map. The date is 12th May 2010. By 2012, the port was handling 55m tonnes of traffic, using 260 trains per week. (R.Humm)

Humber Road Junction

89. No. 56091 enters Immingham reception sidings on 7th August 2002 with a rake of VKA, VGA and VAA vans, forming the 15.08 trip working from Grimsby Docks. The traffic was zinc ingots, bound for Trident Alloys at Bloxwich in the West Midlands. The train would have been routed via Habrough, in order to avoid a reversal at West Marsh. The 40-lever signal box there was in use from 1925 until 1st August 1982. Marshalling Sidings had a box with 44 levers from March 1913 until January 1917. (P.D.Shannon)

Humber Refinery

90. It is 3rd March 2007 and no. 66511 is running past the nine North Sidings. Access was at both ends and a further five loading sidings were on the right. (J.Whitehouse)

Reception Sidings

91. No. 08689 is engaged in shunting duties at Immingham reception sidings on 7th August 2002. At that time, the yard was enjoying a revival thanks to wagonload freight on the EWS Enterprise network, but that revival turned out to be short-lived. (P.D.Shannon)

92. The box is shown lower centre on the left page of the diagram before picture 82 (XXII). It was photographed on 12th May 2010. The Dock then covered 1230 acres, 53 of which were water covered. The box opened on 6th October 1911 and had a massive 97-lever frame. A small panel came in 1967 and a switch panel was worked from 3rd May 1970. (R.Humm)

Motive Power Depot

93. Seen on 19th May 1952 was class 04/8 2-8-0 no. 63802, a type rebuilt by the LNER in 1944. It was later reclassified 04. The water tank stands on legs. The shed was coded 40B and it had two 65ft turntables. (H.C.Casserley)

94. The massive shed is lower right on map XXI and was photographed in about 1960; it had changed little since being built in 1912. There were 120 locomotives allocated here in 1950. It closed to steam in 1966 and still had its massive concrete coaling tower, seen on the left. The diesel depot was built behind the shed. The latter was given over to wagon repairs and demolished in 2008. (D.K.Jones coll.)

95. Left to right are nos 31188 and 47119 on 30th May 1990. EWS took control in 1995 and only fuelling took place here subsequently. Initially, the depot undertook the servicing of engines from distant locations. Diesels were sometimes housed in the old steam shed, from 1999. (M.J.Stretton)

96. Upon opening in 1966, the diesel depot had 90 main line engines and 35 shunters. By 2002, Immingham diesel depot had one of the largest locomotive allocations in the country, including about a quarter of the class 66 fleet. Nos 66166 and 56100 were among the locomotives present on 7th August 2002. The new roof is evident. (P.D.Shannon)

East Junction

97. This is on the right page of the last diagram and we are looking northeast. This and the next picture were taken on 12th May 2010. The Humber International Terminal opened in June 2000. (R.Humm)

98. We are seeing the curves to the facilities east of the locks and are looking north. By 2016, there were over 4m tons of products moved annually by rail from Lindsey Oil Refinery and Humber Oil Refinery. The 1913 box had 72 miniature levers and a small panel was added on 27th September 1981. Closure came on 21st November 2012. (R.Humm)

99. EWS moved regular trainloads of crude oil from Welton to the Simon Storage tank farm at Immingham East, for final delivery by pipeline to Lindsey refinery. No. 56099 shunts loaded TEA tanks at the Simon Storage terminal on 7th August 2002, after forming the 16.07 departure from Welton. This traffic ceased in 2008. (P.D.Shannon)

West Junction

100. This is on the left page of the last map (XXII). This view includes barriers up in the distance and features the windowless toilet at the top of the stairs. The box was in use from 25th March 1912 to 5th September 1979 and housed a 48-lever frame. A switch panel came that day and, on 1st May 2006, another arrived, which was more modern. The thick base walls were added during World War II to resist bomb blasts. (R.Humm)

Mineral Quay

101. No. 08735 shunts vans at Immingham Mineral Quay on 7th August 2002. The traffic was imported paper reels for Stora Enso, which at that time distributed by rail to Selby, Knowsley and Glasgow Deanside. In 2007-08, a £45m 2m ton biofuel plant was constructed, manufacturing biodiesel from vegetable oils. (P.D.Shannon)

Bulk Terminal

102. The rise in imported coal traffic through Immingham prompted the building of Humber International Terminal, a deep-water multi-purpose terminal alongside reclaimed land in the Humber estuary. Phase One of the terminal was completed in 2000 and offered a berth capable of accepting vessels carrying up to 100,000 tonnes of cargo. The new rail siding for Humber International Terminal is pictured on 7th August 2002, shortly before it opened to traffic. (P.D.Shannon)

103. The new coal loading bunker for imported coal is seen in May 2010, with plenty of stairs for the maintenance staff. The oil terminal was opened in 1969 and extended greatly in 1994. Four roll-on/roll-off berths were added in 2006. Two container terminals followed. (R.Humm)

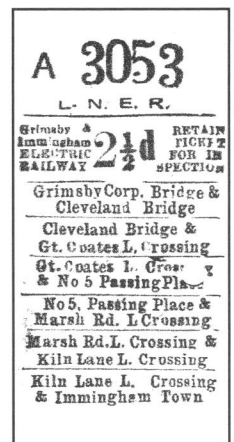

Eastern Jetty

104. The jetty is in the background, behind the office block of the Dock. The line from the Jetty takes a complete semi-circle behind the offices. Terminating close to the circle is the electric railway and one of its cars is standing there. The ship is in the dry dock, which closed in 2001. (R.Humm coll.)

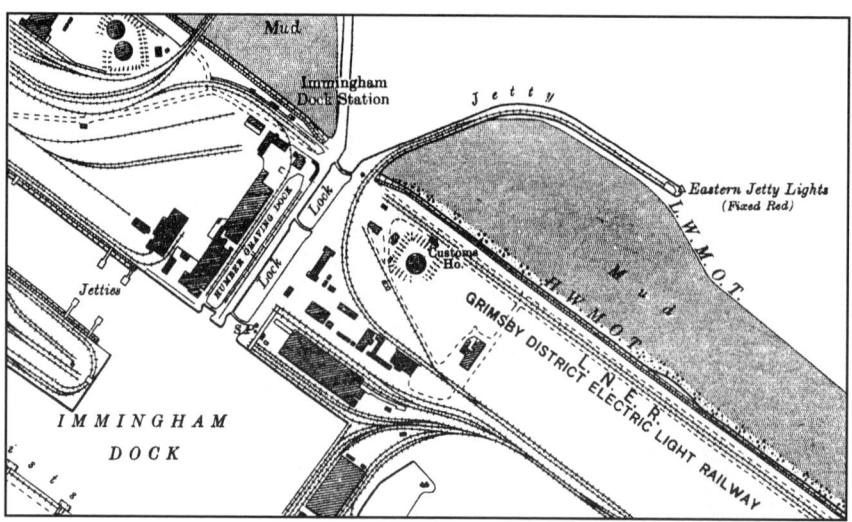

XXIII. The 1932 edition at 6ins to 1 mile shows the details given in caption 104.

105. This is a view along Eastern Jetty with the curve to the shore in the left background. The *SS Orford* is unloading cruise passengers in about 1939 at the platform used exclusively for that purpose. It was never used after that year. Nearest is the chute for luggage. The GCR's vessels focussed on Antwerp, Hamburg and Rotterdam. Later, the LNER cruises were mostly to Scandinavia. (J.Alsop coll.)

Grimsby District Light Railway

106. The journey from Eastern Jetty to Grimsby was 5¾ miles long and a workers' service was provided by the GCR from May 1906. A steam railmotor is standing at the eastern terminus at Pyewipe Road. The public was carried from 3rd November 1910 until the electric line opened on 15th May 1912. Its short life explains the absence of stations from the maps. (J.Alsop coll.)

4. Grimsby & Immingham Electric Light Railway

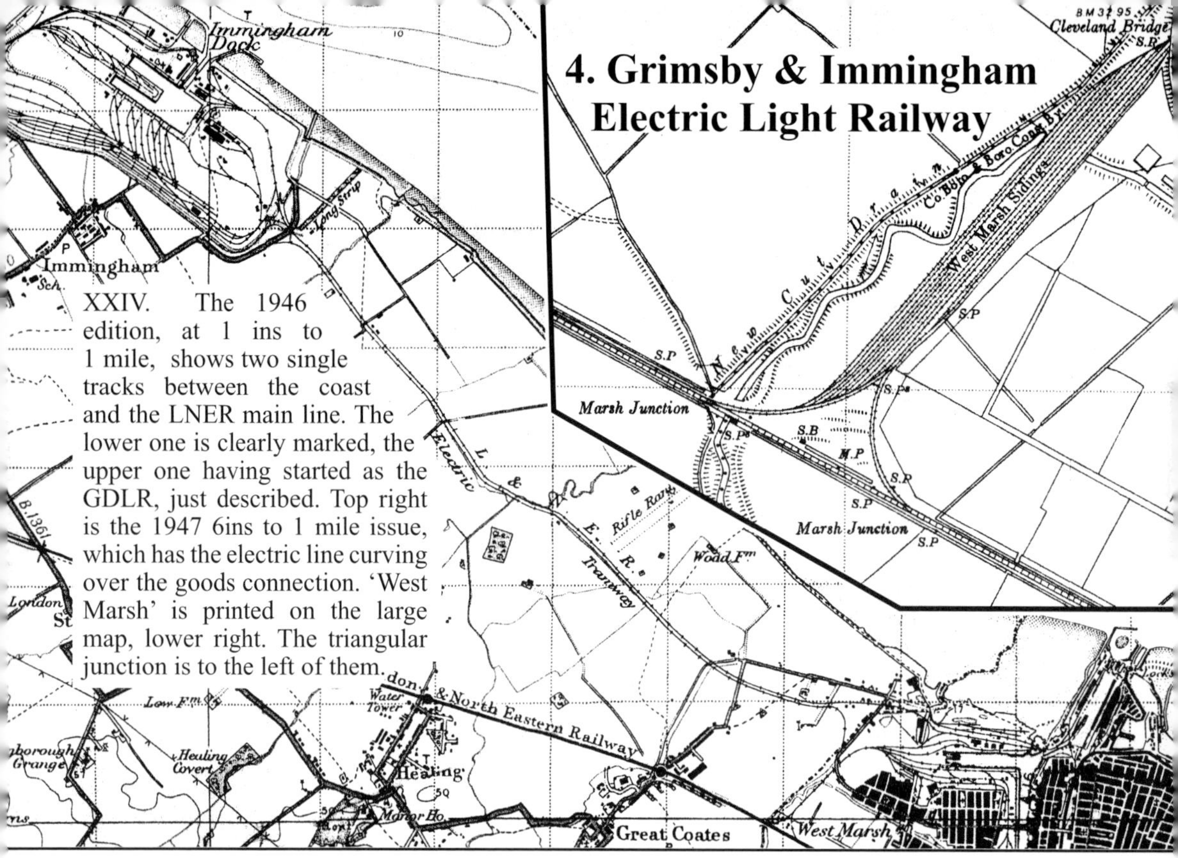

XXIV. The 1946 edition, at 1 ins to 1 mile, shows two single tracks between the coast and the LNER main line. The lower one is clearly marked, the upper one having started as the GDLR, just described. Top right is the 1947 6ins to 1 mile issue, which has the electric line curving over the goods connection. 'West Marsh' is printed on the large map, lower right. The triangular junction is to the left of them.

XXV. This extract is from the 1908 survey and shows the GDLR under construction below the Tile Works (top left). Further south, 'in course of construction' is abbreviated; this was for the electric line. This would cross Pyewipe Road and run the full length of Corporation Road, to terminate at Corporation Bridge. This extract continues west of map III of Grimsby. The Alexandra Dock was developed in 1872-79 for general cargoes: coal exporting and import of Swedish iron ore. As ships grew in size, the new docks at Immingham were developed by the GCR. This left Grimsby to expand with fish traffic.

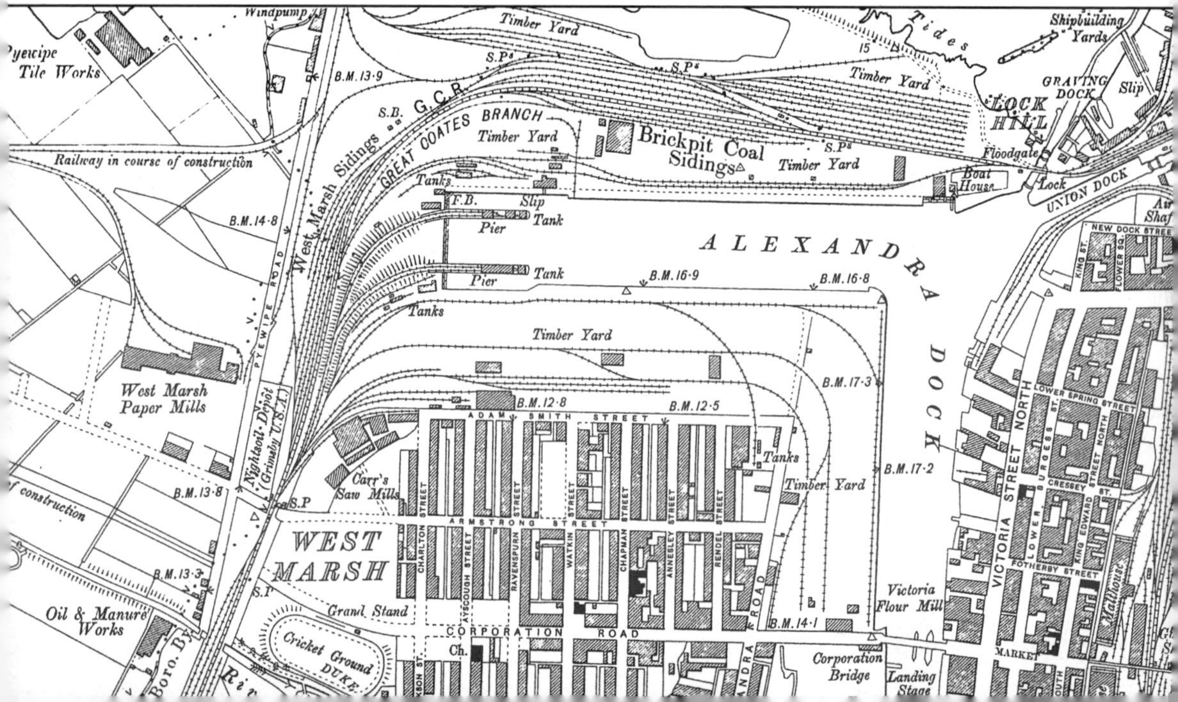

Corporation Bridge

107. We take our journey from east to west, as the railway was named that way. The Grimsby terminus was at the east end of Corporation Street - the moving bridge is evident. Cars 1, 11, 14 and 4 are resting on 21st June 1953. The power station closed in November 1957 and the National Grid became the source. (J.H.Meredith/Online Transport Archive)

108. Some bridge details are evident as no. 13 waits to return on 9th May 1946. The right pole is on the live wire, while the left one is retained under the hook by its springs, evident near the roof. The 1872 hand-operated swing bridge was unfit for the tramway when it opened in 1912. When the bridge was replaced in 1928, traffic was in decline and so no extension was laid. NE instead of LNER on the body was a wartime economy measure. A green livery was introduced in 1951. (H.C.Casserley)

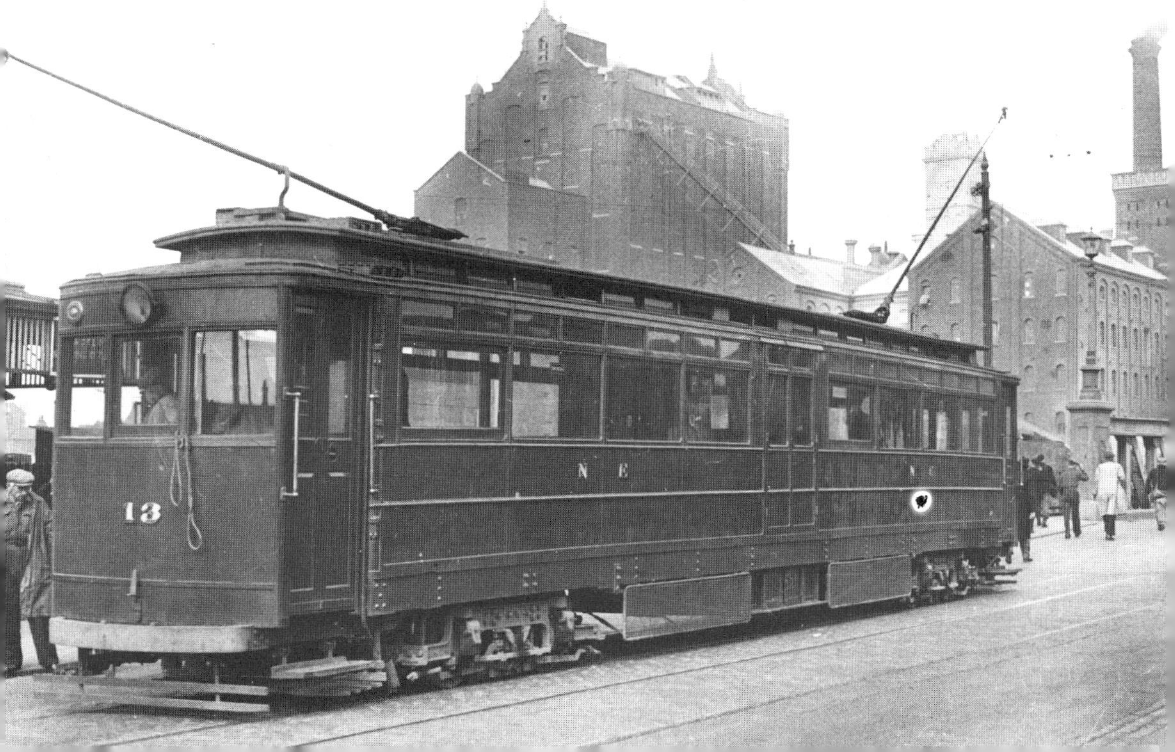

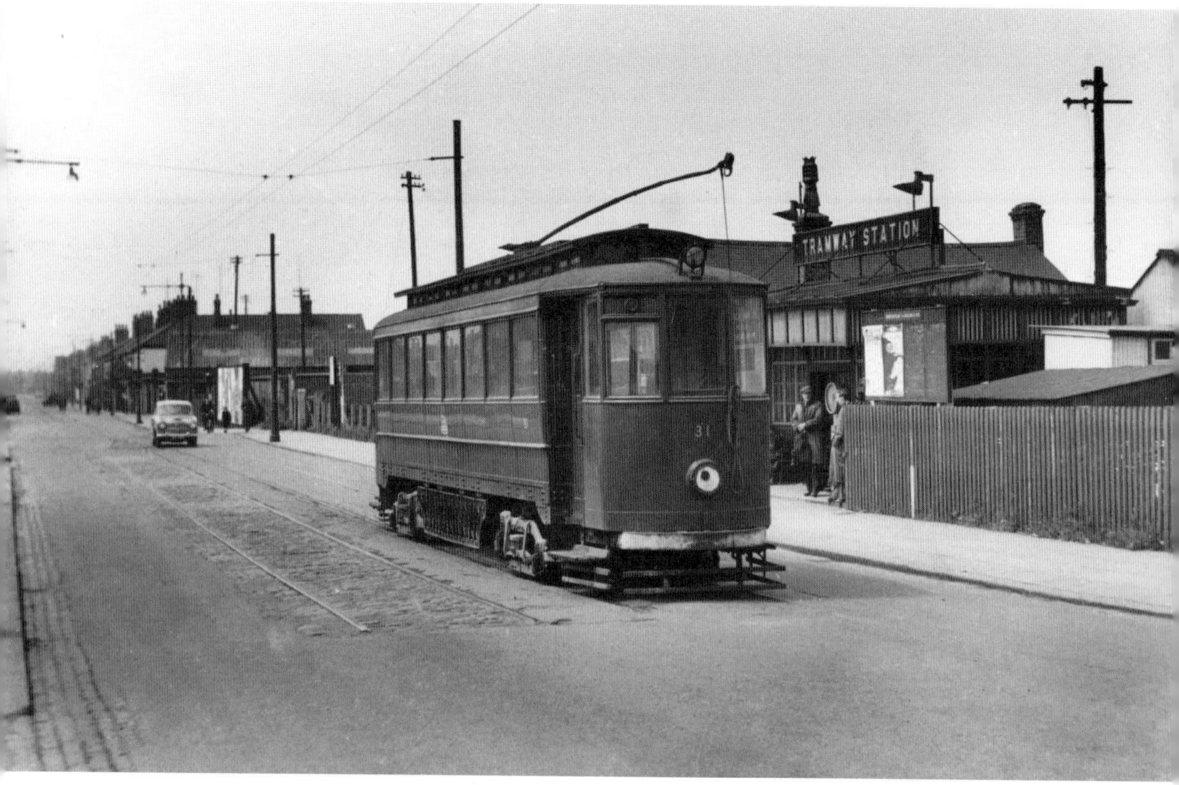

109. The rails and adjacent granite blocks came to an end here, at the east end of Corporation Road. The only locations to have shelters for passengers were here and at the other terminus. No. 31 and some others had only one trolley pole. It meant that the conductor had to walk halfway across the road with its rope to turn it. (R.Humm coll.)

Y 0424
L. N. E. R.
Grimsby & Immingham Electric Ry
Retain Ticket for Inspection.
CHEAP RETURN TICKET
Outward Available any day by any car after 7-45 Return on day of issue only by any car
Grimsby Corp. B'ge, to Immingham Town or Dock and vice versa
This Ticket must be punched in the section indicating the day of issue and must be shewn on demand, and is issued subject to the Conditions on the Company's Bills & Notices.
FARE 1/1
SAT. | FRI. | THUR. | WED. | TUES. | MON. | SUN.
RETURN JOURNEY
OUTWARD JOURNEY
FRI. | THUR. | WED. | TUES. | MON. | SUN.

T 1224
L. N. E. R.
Grimsby & Immingham Electric Railway
2½d
RETAIN TICKET FOR INSPECTION
Grimsby Corp Bridge & Cleveland Bridge
Cleveland Bridge & Gt. Coates L. Crossing
Gt. Coates L. Crossing & No. 5, Passing Place
No. 5, Passing Place & Marsh Rd. L. Crossing
Marsh Rd. L. Crossing & Kiln Lane L. Crossing
Kiln Lane L. Crossing & Immingham Town

K 9351
L. N. E. R.
Grimsby & Immingham Electric Railway
4½d
RETAIN TICKET FOR INSPECTION
Grimsby Corp Bridge & Gt. Coates L. Crossing
Beeson Street & St. Coates L. Crossing
Cleveland Bridge & No. 5, Passing Place
No. 5, Passing Place & Kiln Lane L. Crossing
Marsh Rd. L. Crossing & Immingham Town
Immingham Town & Immingham Dock

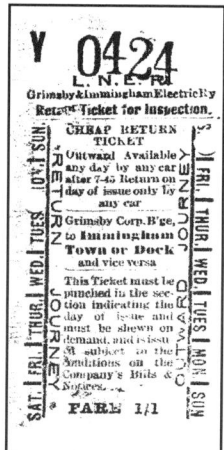

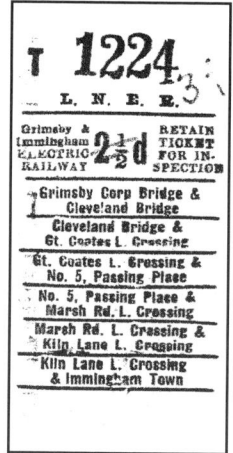

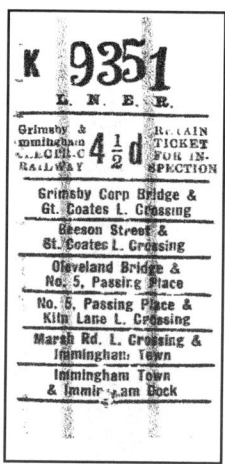

110. The facilities in 1954 included a parcels office, a booking office, a tea room, a waiting room and two personal weighing machines. Weight details came up on the large dials, for all to see. One penny had to be inserted for the pleasure. (R.M.Casserley)

Corporation Road

111. The route was mostly single track, the passing loop being invisibly spring loaded and thus automatic. There were eight loops until 1917 and six thereafter. We see no. 14 in Corporation Road, which joined Gilbey Road. A connection across the river might have stopped the Corporation trams ceasing in 1937. (Unknown)

Cleveland Bridge

112. The bridge is top on the inset on map XXIV and part of one wall is seen here on 9th May 1946. On the left is an overhead cable, which is seen to supply current to both overhead conductors. The return current ran through the rails. The voltage was 500DC. This was the eastern terminus from June 1956. (H.C.Casserley)

113. Passengers are having to walk over the bridge during track repairs in June 1950. Evidence in the foreground shows that conventional grooved tramway rail was not used here. The trolley wheels were replaced by swivelling carbon shoes in 1940, to reduce sparks. (R.Humm coll.)

Pyewipe Depot

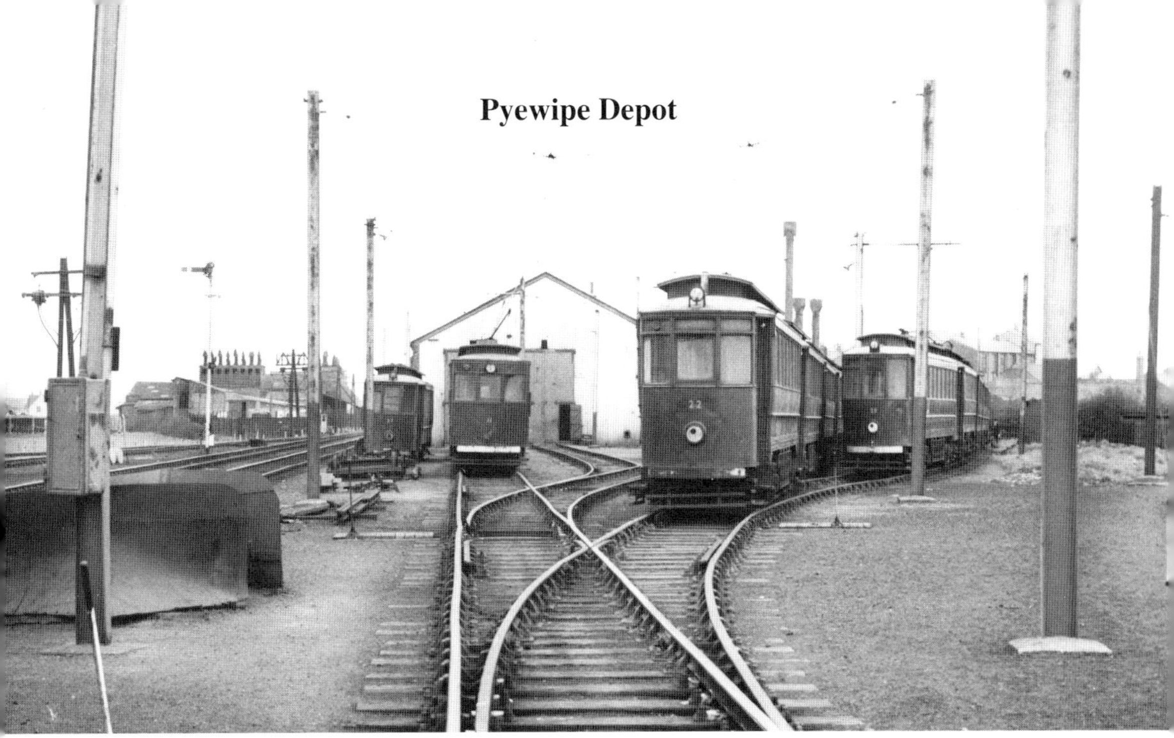

114. Only three cars could be under cover at the same time. The site was also known as Cleveland Bridge Works. Resting on 5th May 1960 are nos 27, 11, 22 and 28. Museums later received three cars: Crich, no. 20, Beamish, no. 26 and NRM, no. 14. (P.J.Kelley)

GRIMSBY, – **Richardson's Victoria Commercial House,** 135, Victoria Street. Central for Commercial Gentlemen Terms Moderate.

GRIMSBY.—**Clarence** Commercial Hotel, Old Market Place. One minute from Town Station and G.P.O. Dinners from 12 till 3. Under Personal Supervision.
Proprietress, M. DAVIS.

GRIMSBY.—**Harman's** Commercial Hotel (Unlicensed), Wellowgate corner. Near Town Station and G.P.O. Every accommodation for Commercial Gentlemen, Visitors, Tourists and Cyclists. Commercial Room greatly enlarged, and New Commercial Entrance. Home comforts. Hot and cold baths.
A. G. HARMAN, PROPRIETOR.

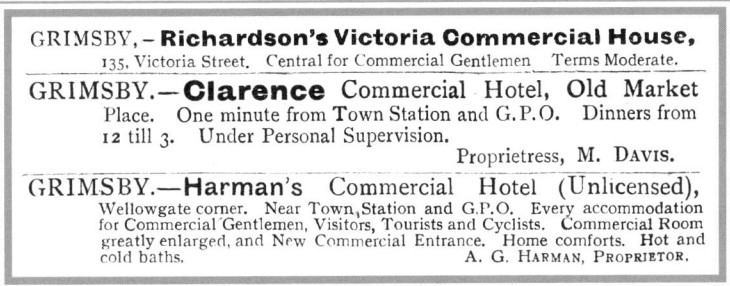

Extract from *Good Lines*, the Temperance Society listing, 1911.

XXVI. The 1931 edition shows 'Engine Shed'. The electric running line and Loop 2 are near the lower fence and the depot is on the right. The GDLR route of 1906 is at the top.

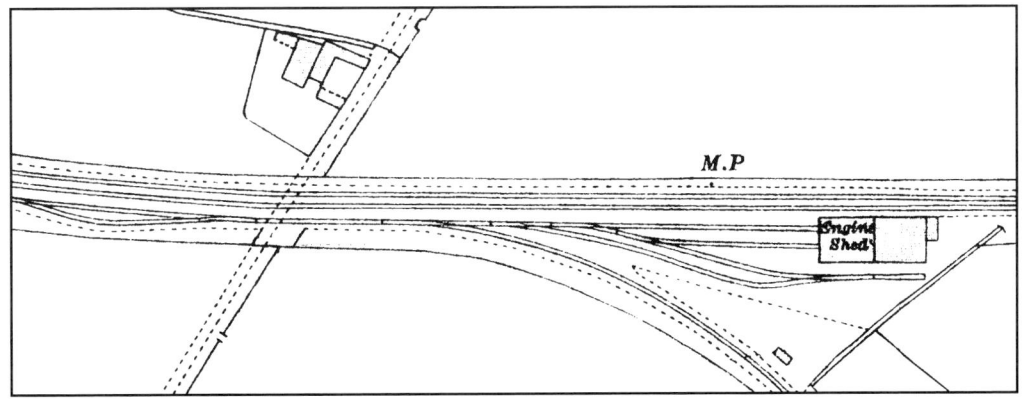

115. Seen on the same day is no. 11, together with a tram showing the BR logo, only possible on this line. I term it the 'Lion & Monocycle'. Cars 1-8 came from Brush for the start, nos 9-12 were from Dick, Kerr and four long cars (13-16) arrived in 1915 from Brush. These details vary from sources. (P.J.Kelley)

116. No. 17 was the maintenance car and it became BR no. DE 30224. Spoked wheels support the overhead maintenance unit. It went to Crich Tramway Village as an exhibit. Car no. 5 had earlier done this work. The low headlamps were mostly moved to the roof, but this car gained two. (R.Humm coll.)

117. High tides coupled with a very severe storm caused many deaths and much damage on the North Sea coast in January 1953. The erosion near Passing Place 8 is under repair, as passengers walk by to join another car. Your scribe was one of many university students ordered to help manually with repairs along the coast. (J.H.Meredith/Online Transport Archive)

Immingham Town

118. No. 2 is seen in its LNER livery (a teak finish) with the conductor gripping the pole rope. Three cars came from Newcastle-upon-Tyne in 1948 and were numbered 6, 7 & 8, but they were withdrawn in 1952. Traffic increased and so 18 came from Gateshead, becoming nos 17-33. Only 17 entered service, as a crane fell on one during unloading; hence the number series 17-33 being only 17 tramcars. The line from Grimsby to here was opened on 15th May 1912. Trams had to reverse here to reach the terminus. (R.Humm coll.)

119. The bridge over the Grimsby District Light Railway is on the left. Cars nos 14 and 12 are on the double track to Grimsby, on the right. It soon became single. We are looking towards the coast here. The route from here to the terminus came into use on 17th November 1913. (R.Humm coll.)

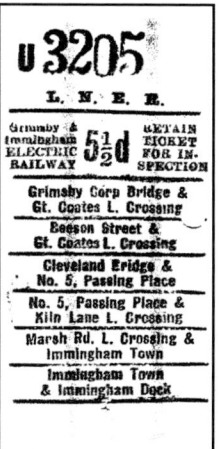
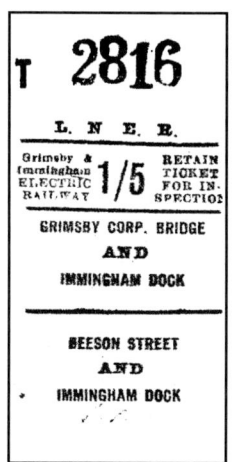

Immingham Dock Terminus

120a. The tracks end here, as does the power supply. The small porcelain insulators at the top of the poles were for telephone wires. No. 12 is resting on 21st June 1953, while no. 26 appears to be loading. (R.J.Harley coll.)

120b. We see no. 4 at the terminus on 24th June 1961, with evidence of the locks beyond. Little passenger service was on offer at this station, but the joy of the journey could be anticipated here. It was widely known as 'The Clickety'. Cars were often stored here between busy periods, as seen. They frequently ran in groups at peak times, sometimes seven at once. (R.M.Casserley)

GRIMSBY & IMMINGHAM ELECTRIC RAILWAY

PASSENGER FARES

	Ordinary single s. d.	Special Cheap Day Return s. d.
CLEVELAND BRIDGE and		
Great Coates Level Crossing	3	—
No. 5 Passing Place	5	—
Marsh Road Level Crossing	8	1 2
Kiln Lane, Stallingborough	11	1 8
Immingham Town	1 1	2 1
Immingham Dock	1 3	2 1
GREAT COATES LEVEL CROSSING and		
No. 5 Passing Place	5	—
Marsh Road Level Crossing	8	1 2
Kiln Lane, Stallingborough	8	1 2
Immingham Town	10	1 6
Immingham Dock	1 1	1 10
No. 5 PASSING PLACE and		
Marsh Road Level Crossing	5	—
Kiln Lane, Stallingborough	5	—
Immingham Town	8	1 2
Immingham Dock	10	1 6
MARSH ROAD LEVEL CROSSING and		
Kiln Lane, Stallingborough	3	—
Immingham Town	5	—
Immingham Dock	8	1 2
KILN LANE, STALLINGBOROUGH and		
Immingham Town	3	—
Immingham Dock	8	1 2
IMMINGHAM TOWN and		
Immingham Dock	5	—

AVAILABILITY

Ordinary tickets
    Single tickets ... 3 days
    Return tickets at double single fare ... 3 months

Children under three years of age are conveyed free, and those of three and under fourteen at half-fares.

Special Cheap Day return tickets

Outward and return—by any car on day of issue. (Note: Passengers travelling to their place of work on one day and whose hours of duty end after midnight, will be allowed to return without extra payment). Children under three years of age are conveyed free, and those of three and under fourteen at half-fares.

Season Tickets

Particulars of rates and conditions are obtainable at Grimsby (Cleveland Bridge) and Immingham or from the Traffic Manager, 26/28 Newland, Lincoln (Tel. Lincoln 26352).

Conditions of Issue.—These tickets are issued subject to the British Transport Commission's published Regulations and Conditions applicable to British Railways exhibited at their stations, and obtainable free of charge at station booking offices.

BRITISH RAILWAYS

LINCOLNSHIRE ROAD CAR COMPANY LIMITED

GRIMSBY — CLEETHORPES TRANSPORT

TIME AND FARE TABLES OF TRAMWAY STEAM TRAIN AND BUS SERVICES

GRIMSBY & IMMINGHAM ELECTRIC RAILWAY

Peak Period Service from 28th September, 1959.

WEEKDAYS ONLY

FROM GRIMSBY (CLEVELAND BRIDGE)		FROM IMMINGHAM DOCK	
DEPARTURES		DEPARTURES	
a.m.	noon	a.m.	p.m.
5.30	12.00 S.O.	5.55	1.03 S.O.
6.00	p.m.	6.23	1.33 S.O.
6.30	12.30 S.O.	6.53	2.03 S.O.
6.50	1.00 S.O.	7.33	4.03 S.X.
7.00	1.30 S.O.	8.03	4.35 S.X.
7.15	3.30 S.X.	8.31	4.53 S.X.
7.25	4.32 S.X.	9.03	5.03 S.X.
7.30	5.00 S.X.	11.33 S.O.	5.21 S.X.
8.00	5.30 S.X.	p.m.	5.33 S.X.
8.30		12.03 S.O.	6.03 S.X.
8.38		12.33 S.O	

S.O.—Saturdays only.   S.X.—Saturdays excepted.

The Cars stop at

IMMINGHAM TOWN

and by request at

GREAT COATES LEVEL CROSSING   No. 5 PASSING PLACE
MARSH ROAD LEVEL CROSSING   KILN LANE, STALLINGBOROUGH

THIS SERVICE IS SUBJECT TO REVISION. PARTICULARS OF ANY ALTERATIONS WILL BE ANNOUNCED LOCALLY

A CONNECTING SERVICE OF GRIMSBY—CLEETHORPES TRANSPORT OMNIBUSES WILL CONTINUE TO OPERATE BETWEEN CORPORATION BRIDGE AND CLEVELAND BRIDGE: THE EXISTING NIGHT SERVICE WILL BE DISCONTINUED

MP Middleton Press

EVOLVING THE ULTIMATE RAIL ENCYCLOPEDIA

Easebourne Midhurst GU29 9AZ. Tel:01730 813169

www.middletonpress.co.uk email:info@middletonpress.co.uk
A-978 0 906520 B- 978 1 873793 C- 978 1 901706 D-978 1 904474
E - 978 1 906008 F - 978 1 908174 G - 978 1 910356

All titles listed below were in print at time of publication - please check current availability by looking at our website - *www.middletonpress.co.uk* or by requesting a Brochure which includes our *LATEST* RAILWAY TITLES also our TRAMWAY, TROLLEYBUS, MILITARY and COASTAL series

A
Abergavenny to Merthyr C 91 8
Abertillery & Ebbw Vale Lines D 84 5
Aberystwyth to Carmarthen E 90 1
Allhallows - Branch Line to A 62 8
Alton - Branch Lines to A 11 6
Andover to Southampton A 82 6
Ascot - Branch Lines around A 64 2
Ashburton - Branch Line to B 95 4
Ashford - Steam to Eurostar B 67 1
Ashford to Dover A 48 2
Austrian Narrow Gauge D 04 3
Avonmouth - BL around D 42 5
Aylesbury to Rugby D 91 3

B
Baker Street to Uxbridge D 90 6
Bala to Llandudno E 87 1
Banbury to Birmingham D 27 2
Banbury to Cheltenham E 63 5
Bangor to Holyhead F 01 7
Bangor to Portmadoc E 72 7
Barking to Southend C 80 2
Barmouth to Pwllheli E 53 6
Barry - Branch Lines around D 50 0
Bartlow - Branch Lines to F 27 7
Bath Green Park to Bristol C 36 9
Bath to Evercreech Junction A 60 4
Beamish 40 years on rails E94 9
Bedford to Wellingborough D 31 9
Berwick to Drem F 64 2
Berwick to St. Boswells F 75 8
B'ham to Tamworth & Nuneaton F 63 5
Birkenhead to West Kirby F 61 1
Birmingham to Wolverhampton E253
Blackburn to Hellifield F 95 6
Bletchley to Cambridge D 94 4
Bletchley to Rugby E 07 9
Bodmin - Branch Lines around B 83 1
Boston to Lincoln F 80 2
Bournemouth to Evercreech Jn A 46 8
Bournemouth to Weymouth A 57 4
Bradshaw's History F18 5
Bradshaw's Rail Times 1850 F 13 0
Bradshaw's Rail Times 1895 F 11 6
Branch Lines series - see town names
Brecon to Neath D 43 2
Brecon to Newport D 16 6
Brecon to Newtown E 06 2
Brighton to Eastbourne A 16 1
Brighton to Worthing A 03 1
Bristol to Taunton D 03 6
Bromley South to Rochester B 23 7
Bromsgrove to Birmingham D 87 6
Bromsgrove to Gloucester D 73 9
Broxbourne to Cambridge F16 1
Brunel - A railtour D 74 6
Bude - Branch Line to B 29 9
Burnham to Evercreech Jn B 68 0

C
Cambridge to Ely D 55 5
Canterbury - BLs around B 58 9
Cardiff to Dowlais (Cae Harris) E 47 5
Cardiff to Pontypridd E 95 6
Cardiff to Swansea E 42 0
Carlisle to Hawick E 85 7
Carmarthen to Fishguard E 66 6
Caterham & Tattenham Corner B251
Central & Southern Spain NG E 91 8
Chard and Yeovil - BLs a C 30 7
Charing Cross to Dartford A 75 8
Charing Cross to Orpington A 96 3
Cheddar - Branch Line to B 90 9
Cheltenham to Andover C 43 7
Cheltenham to Redditch D 81 4
Chester to Birkenhead F 21 5
Chester to Manchester F 51 2
Chester to Rhyl E 93 2
Chester to Warrington F 40 6
Chichester to Portsmouth A 14 7
Clacton and Walton - BLs to F 04 8
Clapham Jn to Beckenham Jn B 36 7
Cleobury Mortimer - BLs a E 18 5
Clevedon & Portishead - BLs to D180
Consett to South Shields E 57 4
Cornwall Narrow Gauge D 56 2
Corris and Vale of Rheidol E 65 9
Coventry to Leicester G 00 5
Craven Arms to Llandeilo E 35 2
Craven Arms to Wellington E 33 8
Crawley to Littlehampton A 34 5
Crewe to Manchester F 57 4
Cromer - Branch Lines around C 26 0
Croydon to East Grinstead B 48 0
Crystal Palace & Catford Loop B 87 1
Cyprus Narrow Gauge E 13 0

D
Darjeeling Revisited F 09 3
Darlington Leamside Newcastle E 28 4
Darlington to Newcastle D 98 2
Dartford to Sittingbourne B 34 3
Denbigh - Branch Lines around F 32 1
Derby to Stoke-on-Trent F 93 2
Derwent Valley - BL to the D 06 7
Devon Narrow Gauge E 09 3
Didcot to Banbury D 02 9
Didcot to Swindon C 84 0
Didcot to Winchester C 13 0
Dorset & Somerset NG D 76 0
Douglas - Laxey - Ramsey E 75 8
Douglas to Peel C 88 8
Douglas to Port Erin C 55 0
Douglas to Ramsey D 39 5
Dover to Ramsgate A 78 9
Drem to Edinburgh G 06 7
Dublin Northwards in 1950s E 31 4
Dunstable - Branch Lines to E 27 7

E
Ealing to Slough C 42 0
Eastbourne to Hastings A 27 7
East Cornwall Mineral Railways D 22 7
East Croydon to Three Bridges A 53 6
Eastern Spain Narrow Gauge E 56 7
East Grinstead - BLs to A 07 9
East Kent Light Railway A 61 1
East London - Branch Lines of C 44 4
East London Line B 80 0
East of Norwich - Branch Lines E 69 7
Effingham Junction - BLs a A 74 1
Ely to Norwich C 90 1
Enfield Town & Palace Gates D 32 6
Epsom to Horsham A 30 7
Eritrean Narrow Gauge E 38 3
Euston to Harrow & Wealdstone C 89 5
Exeter to Barnstaple B 15 2
Exeter to Newton Abbot C 49 9
Exeter to Tavistock B 69 5
Exmouth - Branch Lines to B 00 8

F
Fairford - Branch Line to A 52 9
Falmouth, Helston & St. Ives C 74 1
Fareham to Salisbury A 67 3
Faversham to Dover B 05 3
Felixstowe & Aldeburgh - BL to D 20 3
Fenchurch Street to Barking C 20 8
Festiniog - 50 yrs of enterprise C 83 3
Festiniog 1946-55 E 01 7
Festiniog in the Fifties B 68 8
Festiniog in the Sixties B 91 6
Ffestiniog in Colour 1955-82 F 25 3
Finsbury Park to Alexandra Pal C 02 8
French Metre Gauge Survivors F 88 8
Frome to Bristol B 77 0

G
Galashiels to Edinburgh F 52 9
Gloucester to Bristol D 35 7
Gloucester to Cardiff D 66 1
Gosport - Branch Lines around A 36 9
Greece Narrow Gauge D 72 2
Grimsby - Branch Lines north of G 09 8

H
Hampshire Narrow Gauge D 36 4
Harrow to Watford D 14 2
Harwich & Hadleigh - BLs to F 02 4
Harz Revisited F 62 8
Hastings to Ashford A 37 6
Hawick to Galashiels F 36 9
Hawkhurst - Branch Line to A 66 6
Hayling - Branch Line to A 12 3
Hay-on-Wye - BL around D 92 0
Haywards Heath to Seaford A 28 4
Hemel Hempstead - BLs to D 88 3
Henley, Windsor & Marlow - BLa C77 2
Hereford to Newport D 54 8
Hertford & Hatfield - BLs a E 58 1
Hertford Loop E 71 0
Hexham to Carlisle D 75 3
Hexham to Hawick F 08 6
Hitchin to Peterborough D 07 4
Holborn Viaduct to Lewisham A 81 9
Horsham - Branch Lines to A 02 4
Huntingdon - Branch Line to A 93 2

I
Ilford to Shenfield C 97 0
Ilfracombe - Branch Line to B 21 3
Industrial Rlys of the South East A 09 3
Ipswich to Diss F 81 9
Ipswich to Saxmundham C 41 3
Isle of Man Railway Journey F 94 9
Isle of Wight Lines - 50 yrs C 12 3
Italy Narrow Gauge F 17 8

K
Kent Narrow Gauge C 45 1
Kettering to Nottingham F 82-6
Kidderminster to Shrewsbury E 10 9
Kingsbridge - Branch Line to C 98 7
Kings Cross to Potters Bar E 62 8
King's Lynn to Hunstanton F 58 1
Kingston & Hounslow Loops A 83 3
Kingswear - Branch Line to C 17 8

L
Lambourn - Branch Line to C 70 3
Launceston & Princetown - BLs C 19 2
Leek - Branch Line From G 01 2
Leicester to Burton F 85 7
Lewisham to Dartford A 92 5
Lincoln to Cleethorpes F 56 7
Lincoln to Doncaster G 03 6
Lines around Stamford F 98 7
Lines around Wimbledon B 75 6
Liverpool Street to Chingford D 01 2
Liverpool Street to Ilford C 34 5
Llandeilo to Swansea E 46 8
London Bridge to Addiscombe B 20 6
London Bridge to East Croydon A 58 1
Longmoor - Branch Lines to A 41 3
Looe - Branch Line to C 22 2
Loughborough to Nottingham F 68 0
Lowestoft - BLs around E 40 6
Ludlow to Hereford E 14 7
Lydney - Branch Lines around E 26 0
Lyme Regis - Branch Line to A 45 1
Lynton - Branch Line to B 04 6

M
Machynlleth to Barmouth E 54 3
Maesteg and Tondu Lines E 06 2
Majorca & Corsica Narrow Gauge F 41 3
March - Branch Lines around B 09 1
Market Drayton - BLs around F 67 3
Market Harborough to Newark F 86 4
Marylebone to Rickmansworth D 49 4
Melton Constable to Yarmouth Bch E031
Midhurst - Branch Lines of E 78 9
Midhurst - Branch Lines to F 00 0
Minehead - Branch Line to A 80 2
Mitcham Junction Lines B 01 5
Monmouth - Branch Lines to E 20 8
Monmouthshire Eastern Valleys D 71 5
Moretonhampstead - BL to C 27 7
Moreton-in-Marsh to Worcester D 26 5
Morpeth to Bellingham F 87 1
Mountain Ash to Neath D 80 7

N
Newark to Doncaster F 78 9
Newbury to Westbury C 66 6
Newcastle to Hexham D 69 2
Newport (IOW) - Branch Lines to A 26 0
Newquay - Branch Lines to C 71 0
Newton Abbot to Plymouth C 60 4
Newtown to Aberystwyth E 41 3
Northampton to Peterborough F 92 5
North East German NG D 44 9
Northern Alpine Narrow Gauge F 37 6
Northern France Narrow Gauge C 75 8
Northern Spain Narrow Gauge E 83 3
North London Line B 94 7
North of Birmingham F 55 0
North Woolwich - BLs around C 65 9
Nottingham to Boston F 70 3
Nottingham to Lincoln F 43 7
Nuneaton to Loughborough G 08 1

O
Ongar - Branch Line to E 05 5
Orpington to Tonbridge B 03 9
Oswestry - Branch Lines around E 60 4
Oswestry to Whitchurch E 81 9
Oxford to Bletchley D 57 9
Oxford to Moreton-in-Marsh D 15 9

P
Paddington to Ealing C 37 6
Paddington to Princes Risborough C819
Padstow - Branch Line to B 54 1
Pembroke and Cardigan - BLs to F 29 1
Peterborough to Kings Lynn E 32 1
Peterborough to Lincoln F 89 5
Peterborough to Newark F 72 7
Plymouth - BLs around B 98 5
Plymouth to St. Austell C 63 5
Pontypool to Mountain Ash D 65 4
Pontypridd to Merthyr F 14 7
Pontypridd to Port Talbot E 86 4
Porthmadog 1954-94 - BLa B 31 2
Portmadoc 1923-46 - BLa B 13 8
Portsmouth to Southampton A 31 4
Portugal Narrow Gauge E 67 3
Potters Bar to Cambridge D 70 8
Princes Risborough - BL to D 05 0
Princes Risborough to Banbury C 85 7

R
Railways to Victory C 16 1
Reading to Basingstoke B 27 5
Reading to Didcot C 79 6
Reading to Guildford A 47 5
Redhill to Ashford A 73 4
Return to Blaenau 1970-82 C 64 2
Rhyl to Bangor F 15 4
Rhymney & New Tredegar Lines E 48 2
Rickmansworth to Aylesbury D 61 6
Romania & Bulgaria NG E 23 9
Romneyrail C 32 1
Ross-on-Wye - BLs around E 30 7
Ruabon to Barmouth E 84 0
Rugby to Birmingham E 37 6
Rugby to Loughborough F 12 3
Rugby to Stafford F 07 9
Rugeley to Stoke-on-Trent F 90 1
Ryde to Ventnor A 19 2

S
Salisbury to Westbury B 39 8
Sardinia and Sicily Narrow Gauge F 50 5
Saxmundham to Yarmouth C 69 7
Saxony & Baltic Germany Revisited F 71 0
Saxony Narrow Gauge D 47 0
Seaton & Sidmouth - BLs to A 95 6
Selsey - Branch Line to A 04 8
Sheerness - Branch Line to B 16 2
Shenfield to Ipswich E 96 3
Shrewsbury - Branch Line to A 86 4
Shrewsbury to Chester E 70 3
Shrewsbury to Crewe F 48 2
Shrewsbury to Ludlow E 21 5
Shrewsbury to Newtown E 29 1
Sierra Leone Narrow Gauge D 28 9
Sirhowy Valley Line E 12 3
Sittingbourne to Ramsgate A 90 1
Skegness & Mablethorpe - BL to F 84 0
Slough to Newbury C 56 7
South African Two-foot gauge E 51 2
Southampton to Bournemouth A 42 0
Southend & Southminster BLs E 76 5
Southern Alpine Narrow Gauge F 22 2
Southern France Narrow Gauge C 47 5
South London Line B 46 6
South Lynn to Norwich City F 03 1
Southwold - Branch Line to A 15 4
Spalding - Branch Lines around E 52 9
Spalding to Grimsby F 65 9 6
Stafford to Chester F 34 5
Stafford to Wellington F 59 8
St Albans to Bedford D 08 1
St. Austell to Penzance C 67 3
St. Boswell to Berwick F 44 4
Steaming Through Isle of Wight A 5
Steaming Through West Hants A 69
Stourbridge to Wolverhampton E 16
St. Pancras to Barking D 68 5
St. Pancras to Folkestone E 88 8
St. Pancras to St. Albans C 78 9
Stratford to Cheshunt F 53 6
Stratford-u-Avon to Birmingham D 7
Stratford-u-Avon to Cheltenham C 2
Sudbury - Branch Lines to F 19 2
Surrey Narrow Gauge C 87 1
Sussex Narrow Gauge C 68 0
Swaffham - Branch Lines around F
Swanage to 1999 - BL to A 33 8
Swanley to Ashford B 45 9
Swansea - Branch Lines around F 3
Swansea to Carmarthen E 59 8
Swindon to Bristol C 96 3
Swindon to Gloucester D 46 3
Swindon to Newport D 30 2
Swiss Narrow Gauge C 94 9

T
Talyllyn 60 E 98 7
Tamworth to Derby F 76 5
Taunton to Barnstaple B 60 2
Taunton to Exeter C 82 6
Taunton to Minehead F 39 0
Tavistock to Plymouth B 88 6
Tenterden - Branch Line to A 21 5
Three Bridges to Brighton A 35 2
Tilbury Loop C 86 4
Tiverton - BLs around C 62 8
Tivetshall to Beccles D 41 8
Tonbridge to Hastings A 44 4
Torrington - Branch Lines to B 37 4
Tourist Railways of France G 04 3
Towcester - BLs around E 39 0
Tunbridge Wells BLs A 32 1

U
Upwell - Branch Line to B 64 0
Uttoxeter to Macclesfield G 05 0

V
Victoria to Bromley South A 98 7
Victoria to East Croydon A 40 6
Vivarais Revisited E 08 6

W
Walsall Routes F 45 1
Wantage - Branch Line to D 25 8
Wareham to Swanage 50 yrs D 09 8
Waterloo to Windsor A 54 3
Waterloo to Woking A 38 3
Watford to Leighton Buzzard D 45 6
Wellingborough to Leicester F 73 4
Welshpool to Llanfair E 49 9
Wenford Bridge to Fowey C 09 3
Westbury to Bath B 55 8
Westbury to Taunton C 76 5
West Cornwall Mineral Rlys D 48 7
West Croydon to Epsom B 08 4
West German Narrow Gauge D 93 7
West London - BLs of C 50 5
West London Line B 84 8
West Wiltshire - BLs of D 12 8
Weymouth - BLs A 65 9
Willesden Jn to Richmond B 71 8
Wimbledon to Beckenham C 58 1
Wimbledon to Epsom B 62 6
Wimborne - BLs around A 97 0
Wirksworth - Branch Lines to G 10 4
Wisbech - BLs around C 01 7
Witham & Kelvedon - BLs a E 82 6
Woking to Alton A 59 8
Woking to Portsmouth A 25 3
Woking to Southampton A 55 0
Wolverhampton to Shrewsbury E 44
Wolverhampton to Stafford F 79 6
Worcester to Birmingham D 97 5
Worcester to Hereford D 38 8
Worthing to Chichester A 06 2
Wrexham to New Brighton F 47 5
Wroxham - BLs around F 31 4

Y
Yeovil - 50 yrs change C 38 3
Yeovil to Dorchester A 76 5
Yeovil to Exeter A 91 8
York to Scarborough F 23 9